EQUAL JUSTICE UNDER LAW:

The American Legal System.

By
CARROLL C. MORELAND

Introduction by DAVID F. MAXWELL
President, American Bar Association.

Epilogue by JEFFERSON B. FORDHAM
Dean, University of Pennsylvania Law School.

OCEANA PUBLICATIONS, INC.
New York

Library of Congress Catalog Card Number: 57—12805

To
the memory of
OWEN J. ROBERTS
Exemplar of the finest traditions
of the
American legal profession

TABLE OF CONTENTS

TABLE OF CONTENTS

INTRODUCTION

We are told by the historian, Trevelyan, that as the jury system took shape, after Henry II's Assizes of Clarendon, the English freedman by familiarity gradually gained such self-assurance in legal matters that by the time of the reign of Elizabeth I he was prone to dispute points of law even with lawyers. Amusing instances of this propensity abound in the plays of Shakespeare.

That tradition of joyous legal controversy, brought here in Colonial times, persists throughout the United States today. It is a callow and foolhardy member of the bar, indeed, who ventures a "curb-stone" opinion on a legal question in the presence of bystanders, whether they be insurance adjusters, real estate men, accountants, plumbers, auto mechanics, or just plain vagrants. His venture is certain to produce for him no fee, but only arguments and discomfiture, regardless of the merits of his opinions.

Yet, as lawyers know very well, in the field of law, self-esteem is by no means equal to understanding. The lawyer knows, too, that of all the clients who seek counsel, only a few have more than a glimmering of a perception of the legal consequences of their own, or their adversaries, activities.

So, though plays and motion pictures and the occasional experience of serving on a jury or as a witness, or litigant, has provided a large section of our citizenry with a mental picture of what a court in session, complete with judge, jury, counsel and witnesses, looks like, probably few laymen really grasp the significance of the way in which law and justice is administered by our American court system.

And there is an *American* court system, thanks to the foresight of our forefathers in writing into our national organic law the Bill of Rights, the paramount power of the Supreme Court, the full faith and credit clause, and the clause guaranteeing a republican form of government to the States.

Thanks to those and other wise provisions, our judicial system today is not a variegated conglomeration of independent state tribunals, but rather a pattern of perhaps vari-colored threads woven into a single seamless fabric of law and justice.

This achievement is remarkable, when we consider how systems of law tend to vary according to differences in topography, resources, climate and culture. Certainly in those respects there is enormous variety between one state and another of our United States. In the southwest some states are arid, and Spanish in heritage, with oriental overtones, and a native Indian population. Water rights there would dominate judicial attention. In states rich in minerals, oil, cattle, or timber, the law would perforce emphasize such matters, and the social problems arising out of that sort of economy. In the north, commerce, banking, corporations, and immigration, and in the south, farming and shipping, would tend to be focal points of judicial interest.

Yet the lawyers of America, no matter what state is the locale of their practice, speak to each other in a common language of jurisprudence, which unites them all, even as it sets them apart from lawyers in other lands.

For it is true that the law and the courts of the Federal Government and the several states of the United States, however much they may have resembled in the beginning the English system on which mainly they were modeled, have developed today into a complex sui generis, unlike any other judicial system in the world.

This was inevitable, as our country, largely agricultural when the Constitution was adopted, became what it is today—predominantly urban and industrial. Such a transition, so rapidly consummated, correspondingly changed the concepts and direction of our law, both substantive and procedural.

At first that transition was smoothed, guided, and, except for the war between the states, saved from the outbreak of serious violence, by the imaginative skill and wit of individual lawyers, including illustrious members of Congress and the several state legislatures, who, working within the framework of stare decisis, contrived to mold the law to suit the ever changing times.

When lawyers saw that individually they could not cope successfully with the problems of transition, as it followed its swift and increasingly complicated course, they organized themselves into local, state and national bar associations, dedicated to the improvement of the administration of justice, conformable to the needs of change.

Notable in this endeavor has been the work of the American Bar Association, with its many sections covering every aspect of modern American law. Recently the Association established a special research department, the American Bar Foundation, which will have the special mission of developing solutions to problems which confront the citizen and his courts.

But the administration of justice in this country is not the concern of the lawyer alone; it also is the responsibility of every citizen, whose watchword might well be "equal justice under law." The phrase proclaims not only the equality of everyone before the bar of justice, but also the more important and basic doctrine, that government is one of law, and not of men. Equal justice means the same quality of treatment for the poor as for the rich, for the weak as for the strong, for the one as for the many. It is the duty of every citizen to see to it that this equality is maintained. To do so, he must know the means by which it is accomplished. Such knowledge ordinarily can only come to him from a book such as this, which supplies the information necessary to an understanding of the operation of our legal system, and adds the vital attribute of true understanding to his mental picture of our courts.

DAVID F. MAXWELL

June 1, 1957.

PREFACE

Of all the phases of life in the United States, perhaps the one least clearly understood is the administration of justice through the courts. Yet the legal system of this country is the most important instrument in the maintenance of the American way of life. We have seen personal liberties and freedom diminish and disappear elsewhere in the world in proportion to the decline in the independence of the courts. This brief survey of our legal system has been written in the hope that it will give the reader an understanding of its operation and an appreciation of its merits. Such an appreciation will, it is hoped, create a determination that its benefits may continue, and that its deficiencies may be eliminated.

As is the case with all books, this would never have been completed without the assistance of others. My colleague, Professor John O. Honnold, has been generous with his time and advice. The staff of the Biddle Law Library, and particularly of Paul Gay, Dr. Dorothy Grimm and Nancy Arnold, have been most helpful. Lewis Mayers, whose book, "The American Legal System," gives an elaborate and thorough description of the entire field, supplied information used in the preparation of the manuscript.

CARROLL C. MORELAND

Philadelphia, Pa.
June 15, 1957.

Chapter 1

THE BACKGROUND OF OUR LEGAL SYSTEM

Colonies to Nation

To understand the legal system of the United States, one must recall the situation in which the colonies found themselves after the successful conclusion of the Revolutionary War. We are so accustomed today to think in terms of a dual system of individual states and a central government that we lose sight of the circumstances under which this country was founded.

Prior to 1775 the colonies were entirely separate units of the British empire. They were as separate in their governments and in their very existence as are Australia and Canada today. It happened that their territories were contiguous; they might as well have been miles apart, so far as their governments were concerned. When the colonies began their fight for freedom from the mother country, there was no generally accepted idea as to what the government organization would be, in the event of a successful outcome. It was simply clear that, for the immediate purpose of gaining freedom, there had to be a united effort, since no one colony alone could have overcome the power of England.

The concerted effort of separate colonies to free themselves from the control of England did not of itself and in the first instance contemplate a united country, organized as is the United States today. It is true that there had been a federation of a limited sort formed by Massachusetts, Plymouth, Connecticut and New Haven in 1643, but Rhode Island had not been included because its inhabitants had not been "of the same church fellowship." However, the main objective of the Revolution was to gain freedom. When that had been accomplished, it was obvious that the freed colonies could not exist as separate entities. Given time, England, or any other powerful nation, could come back and take by force of arms the new independent states, one by one. Therefore it became necessary to form a united country which would present a solid front against such an attack.

The Constitutions

The formation of that united country was not easy. Each colony had its own interests. These interests frequently conflicted. Each had its own separate citizenry, loyal to the colony; each had its own individual background. In the process of welding these separate units into one nation it was necessary that concessions be made to each other and to the larger unit, the united country. The Constitution of the United States is the result of these series of concessions and compromises.

It is well to recall that the Constitution formed a new kind of government. No nation had ever before been so organized or by such a means. In 1775 there were thirteen separate colonies; in 1789 there was one nation. That the Constitution has been able to stand up under the strains and stresses of 165 years, without many radical changes, speaks volumes for the ability and foresight of its drafters.

The new nation was achieved by compromising the sovereignty of the individual states and by limiting the powers of the Federal government. The states were jealous of their own rights and bargained sharply for their preservation. The Federal government was granted only those powers which were necessary to run a central government. Under the Constitution, the Federal government was given the power to lay and collect taxes, to regulate commerce among the states, to coin monies, declare war, borrow money, establish post offices, raise and support armies, provide a navy, constitute tribunals inferior to the Supreme Court and provide uniform laws respecting naturalization and bankruptcy. Other powers were reserved to the states.

It was clear that this new country required dual systems, in order that it might function. On the legislative side, there had to be state legislatures, to enact laws to govern those phases of life which were not under the control of Congress. The strong feeling of sovereignty in the states which necessitated a dual legislative system indicated that there must also be an independent court system within each state. It was apparent that there must also be some forum which could disinterestedly decide contests between states and, more important, between citizens of different states. It was clear that no "sovereign" state would permit the courts of another state to decide a controversy which involved one of its own citizens. It was equally clear that when there was a controversy between states, there had to be some neutral court to decide such matters. These matters were discussed at the Constitutional Convention, and decided in the manner under which we now live.

All of the rebelling colonies had had to form some kind of government during the period of the Revolution. They adopted constitutions for this purpose, and all of them provided for a division between the legislative, the executive and the judicial powers. They had had their fill of governors overruling the decisions of their legislative assemblies and their courts. Their experience, prior to the Revolution, insofar as the courts were concerned, had been that the executive or the legislative branches of the colonial government had interfered with the processes of the judicial branch. It was paramount with them that this should not be repeated in their own independent governments. They therefore insisted that there should be separation of these three powers. The Constitution of the United States, following the pattern of the constitutions of the states, contains provisions which carry out this idea. Separate sections deal with these three types of power.

This feeling regarding the separation of the three departments, so strong in 1789, still exists, as witness the public's reaction to the proposal of President Franklin D. Roosevelt to enlarge the Supreme Court. Opposition to that proposal stemmed in large part from the conviction of the people that the executive and the legislative departments should not interfere with the courts. It is interesting to note that, although the legislative bodies were highly regarded at the time of the forming of this country, they were also regarded as possible threats to the independence of the judiciary. Several of the original state constitutions, as well as the Constitution of the United States, provided that the compensation of judges should not be diminished during their terms of office. Courts were not to be coerced by legislative threats of salary reductions!

An Independent Judiciary

The constitutions of the original states for the most part carried over into the new era of government their colonial courts, which were named as the repositories of the judicial power. Even though the original colonies had all been set up by the home country, there had been considerable variations in the charters and powers granted to the colonial governments. This had resulted in differences in their courts, so that there were really thirteen distinct systems, even though they all stemmed from the same English system. In addition to the courts which were named in their constitutions, the states provided for such additional courts as their legislatures might from time to time establish. As additional states were formed, the citizens of each new state adopted that system of courts which seemed to them to be the most satisfactory, in view of the locale and the predominant thought of the area. As a result, there is a great variety of systems in the 48 states today, but all are based on the state constitutions, and are as independent of the legislative and executive branches of the government as it is possible to be.

The drafters of the state constitutions had the advantage of the history of the colonies in preparing the sections on the judiciary. But the framers of the Constitution of the United States had nothing to serve as a model; there had been no court system which included all of the colonies. Therefore they had to create a judicial system. Wisely they created only one court by name. The judicial power of the United States, under the terms of Article III, Sec. 1 of the

Constitution, was "vested in one Supreme Court, and in such inferior courts, as the Congress may, from time to time, ordain and establish." At the time the Constitution of the United States was drafted, the judges of all the states were appointed either by the governor or by the legislature, and in nine of these states, they held office for life. How the Federal Judges were to be selected was a matter of considerable debate. The matter was settled in Article II, Sec. 2 of the Constitution: the President "shall nominate, and by and with the advice and consent of the Senate, appoint . . . judges of the Supreme Court, and all other officers of the United States . . ." The term of the Federal judge was, and still is, "during good behavior."

The Law of the Land

The problem of the kinds of court systems which the new states should have was settled by the adoption or adaptation of the ones which had existed in 1775. The answer to the question of what should be the law of the states was relatively simple. The colonies had been founded or had been under the control of England for over one hundred years. The law which was in force in the colonies at the outbreak of the Revolution was English. The judges looked to the English courts for their precedents; their decisions were subject to final review in England. The English system of law was the only one they knew. Any laws which were adopted by the colonial legislative assemblies were subject to approval by the Crown, and the statutes of the King and Parliament, where applicable, were the law of the colonies. Hence, when it came to declaring what was to be the law of the states, the state constitutions adopted the common law and the statutes of England as of the date of the Revolution. Thus the new states started their existence with a great heritage of law and legal concepts.

What was to be the law of the United States, as distinct from that of various states, was not so easy to determine. It has always been clear that the acts of Congress are the law of the United States which the courts, both state and Federal, enforce. But in cases which do not involve Federal statutes or the application of the law of a particular state, the Federal courts have generally followed the precedents of the common law of England, with such adaptations as the situation might demand.

SELECTED READINGS

For other material, see Bibliography, page 121.

Andrews, Charles McLean. The colonial period in American history. New Haven, Yale university press, 1934. 4v.

The Federalist; a commentary on the Constitution of the United States. New York, Dunne, 1901.

Kinane, Charles Herman. A first book on Anglo-American law. Indianapolis, Boss-Merrill, 1952.

Warren, Charles. The making of the Constitution. Boston, Little Brown, 1928.

Chapter 2

CONSTITUTIONAL GUARANTIES

In the preceding chapter we have examined the background and constitutional provisions pertinent to creating the legal systems of this country. But nothing was said about the guaranties in the state and Federal constitutions which protect the rights of the citizen in his every day life. It is one thing to provide for a system to administer justice; it is quite different, and perhaps more vital, to define and protect the rights of the citizens who make up the states and the nation. It is fortunate that the founders of this country saw to it that the fundamental rights of the citizens were set out in the constitutions of the states and of the United States, and provided that these rights should be inviolate.

State Bills of Rights

Under the British, the colonies had not enjoyed those rights which they were to describe in their constitutions as "great and essential principles of liberty and free government." In fact, it was the violation of what they considered to be their rights and freedom which caused the conflict of 1775. With the outbreak of hostilities, Virginia was the first colony to urge the Continental Congress to declare the freedom and independence of the colonies, and its Convention adopted, on June 12, 1776, the famous "Virginia Declaration of Rights." This Declaration served as a guide for the other colonies, and by 1784 all but Connecticut and Rhode Island had either adopted a Bill of Rights as a specific part of their constitutions, or had incorporated similar provisions in the body of their constitutions.

Since the formation of the United States by the thirteen colonies, thirty-five states have been added to the union. The exigencies under which the original colonies adopted their "Bills of Rights" were not present when these additional states were added. Yet the fact that all of them have seen fit to include in their governmental framework such a declaration is a clear indication that the people of the states of the United States have been determined that their own state governments will not transgress these "great and essential principles of liberty and free government", of which the Virginia Declaration was the first formalized expression.

Federal Bill of Rights

During the drafting of the proposed constitution of the United States, the principle concern of the delegates was the framework of the new national government, and the question of a strong central government versus strong state governments was the main cause for debate. The liberties and freedoms of the individual citizens were not of so much moment, since these presumably had been taken care of by the state constitutions. However, some of the state conventions, called to ratify the Federal constitution, expressed "a desire, in order to prevent misconstruction or abuse of its powers, that further declaratory and restrictive clauses should be added, and as extending the ground of public confidence in the Government will best insure the beneficent ends of its institution."* The first session of the First Congress therefore submitted twelve proposed amendments to the Constitution to the states for adoption. Ten of these were ratified by eleven states and were declared in force on December 15, 1791. These first ten amendments, similar in the main to the Virginia Declaration, are commonly referred to as the Federal Bill of Rights, and serve as a protection against *Federal* action.

Civil Liberty in the United States

A reading of these Bills of Rights gives a summary of the history of the period preceding the Revolution. None of the rights and privileges protected by them had been inviolate prior to the fight for freedom. It was the violation of these

*Preamble to the Resolution of Congress, September 25, 1789.

rights which had touched off hostilities. When the battle had been won, the citizens of the new states and country were determined that these rights would not be taken away from them. To insure this, the Bills of Rights were adopted.*

These "principles of liberty and good government" thus sought to be protected fall into three categories—civil liberty, personal rights and civil rights. Using the Federal Bill of Rights as our text, let us first examine those in the field of civil liberty. The First Amendment protects perhaps the most important freedoms, those of the mind and intellect. It declares that Congress shall make no law respecting an establishment of religion or prohibiting the free exercise thereof. This provision had a two-fold background. On the one hand, there were colonies in which the established religious sect derived advantages from its favored position. On the other hand, the supporters of the prevailing sect in some colonies had placed limitations on those not of that belief, and in some instances non-belief had been the cause of persecution, penalties and expulsion. It was to prevent such occurrences that the states and the United States provided against the establishment of any religion and gave their citizens freedom to follow their consciences in the choice of religious belief.

The right to express views contrary to those of the rulers of the colonies had been seriously threatened and often denied. The colonists had seen their neighbors imprisoned for expressing views not in conformity with those of the colonial governments, and for publishing criticisms of their actions. The right to freely criticize the government was regarded as a means of keeping that government amenable to the wishes of the citizens: hence freedom of speech and freedom of the press were considered as indispensable in the new country. These freedoms are as vital today as they were in 1791, and their protection is equally necessary. In times of stress and tension, such as the world is experiencing, the expression of views contrary to the prevailing ones is always unpopular. It is not a far step from unpopularity

_____

For text, see Appendix A, page 83.

to repression. Freedom to express one's views, whether in speech or in print, is an essential principle of liberty, and its protection must be vigilantly maintained. "I disapprove of what you say but I will defend to the death your right to say it" is as valid now as it was 200 years ago.

Coupled with these freedoms, in the minds of the colonists, was the right of the citizens to assemble and to discuss matters which concerned them. From time to time local governmental agencies have attempted to prevent gatherings of persons whose views were antagonistic to their own: provisions of the constitutions have protected those persons and enabled them to enjoy the freedom of assembly, and have afforded them an opportunity to express their views in public.

Protection of Personal Rights

The Seventh Amendment provided for jury trials in suits at common law, where the amount in controversy exceeds twenty dollars. This right to a civil jury trial, which is also found in state constitutions, is limited in scope. In those kinds of suits in which jury trials were never had, such as proceedings in equity, this right does not exist. What the colonists were protecting was the right which they always had had, and they were not attempting to enlarge it.

The colonists had suffered some "requisitioning" for the King's use, of all kinds of property. They provided, in the Fifth Amendment, that no private property was to be taken for public use without just compensation. When private property, whether personal property or real estate, is needed for public use, the interest of the public is paramount over that of the individual owner, and the government or its agents may take the property. However, the owner must be adequately compensated for his loss, and this provision is his guaranty.

But it is in the realm of criminal law that we find the strongest expression of fear of the infringement of personal rights and the most specific restrictions against their violation. Here again the recital of the "principles of liberty and free government," as contained in the constitutions, gives us a good idea of the conditions under which the colonists had lived. The Bill of Rights of the Federal Constitution provides protection, at the hands of the Federal government, against a series of abuses which had enraged the colonists. The Bills of Rights of the various states for the most part provide the same protection to the citizen against action by his state government. Thus the rights for which the colonists had fought are imbedded in the documents which form the foundation of our system of government.

The rights in criminal matters, dealt with in the Federal Bill of Rights, are indeed worthy of notice. The Fourth Amendment is intended to protect the citizen against unreasonable searches and seizures, and provides for the proper mode of procedure. This amendment recalls to mind the picture of colonial authorities invading a home and ransacking it in the hope of uncovering evidence of some offense against the government. The officers often acted without any search warrant at all, and even when they were in possession of a warrant, the warrant was frequently issued upon suspicion only. In 1789 it was not contended, nor has it ever been, that a house cannot be searched under any circumstances. The Fourth Amendment was written to protect the citizens against *unreasonable* conduct on the part of officers, and specifies the basis upon which warrants of arrest and search are to be issued to Federal officers.

Warrants are not issued on mere suspicion, but the officer must have probable cause to ask for its issuance. Moreover, the application for a warrant must be sworn to or affirmed: the requirement of an oath or affirmation acts as a deterrent to ill-advised actions. Specificity with respect to the description of the place to be searched and of the things to be seized demands proper preparation of the case on the part of the authorities. The Federal courts are strict in their interpretation of this amendment: a Federal warrant directed at the seizure of untaxed liquor does not allow the use as evidence of unlawfully possessed narcotics found on the premises searched. Although this may seem to be extreme, a possible alternative could well be just that type of action which the provision is intended to prevent.

These proscriptions are closely allied to the provision of
the Fifth Amendment that no one can be compelled to be a
witness against himself. Use of materials, which had been
improperly seized, as evidence is regarded by the Federal
courts as in violation of this privilege against self-incrimination. The privilege had its origin in England as a means
of preventing forced confessions from the accused. Whether
the accused is guilty or not, the privilege is one which protects him from over-zealous prosecutors. Like many privileges, it can be waived, as when a defendant takes the witness stand to testify in his own defense. Clearly he is then
subject to questioning which might prove detrimental to
his interests, but that chance has been a result of his choice.

The Fifth Amendment further provides that "no one shall
be held to answer for a capital or other infamous crime
unless on a presentment or indictment of a Grand Jury."
This requirement is a means of preventing vexatious and
unwarranted prosecutions, common during the pre-Revolu-
tionary times. Although the grand jury hears only the evidence of the prosecution in arriving at its decision, the
prosecution must convince it that this evidence, taken by
itself, justifies the trial of the accused. Allied with this provision is one that no one shall "be twice put in jeopardy of
life or limb." Experience again was the instructor of the
new nation: partisan and biased governments, angered at
a finding of "Not guilty" by a trial jury, had had a defendant re-tried more than once, each time hoping for a conviction. Such abuses of the processes of the law was ended
by this provision: prosecution cannot be used for persecution.

The final provision of the Fifth Amendment is one which
is as important as any: no one can be convicted without
"due process of law." This requirement concerns itself not
only with the procedure by which a statute is enacted or
enforced, but also with the substance of the act itself. The
gist of "due process" in the criminal field is a fair trial under
a valid statute. "Due process" may be violated in the conduct of the trial, as in the case of a jury panel arbitrarily
selected so as to exclude certain social or ethnic groups,

or by the criminal statute under which the defendant is being tried, as in the case of a statute beyond the powers of Congress to enact. The requirement of due process is salutary, as a protection against unwarranted interference with a defendant's right to a fair trial under proper and accepted standards.

The Sixth Amendment sets out the rights of the accused during the course of the trial. The accused is entitled to a speedy and public trial. The colonists had learned from experience that the Crown was not always in a hurry to try a defendant: if he were not out on bail, delay of trial was as good as conviction and sentence. Control of the time of trial is ordinarily in the hands of the prosecution, and this provision was introduced to prevent harassment of the accused by an unfriendly prosecutor. Public trials had not always been the rule, either in the colonies or in England, and the colonists were aware that the best way to assure justice was to keep its administration in the searchlight of publicity. Although Article III of the Constitution provided that all criminal trials should be by jury and be held in the state where the crimes were committed, the Sixth Amendment restricted them further by requiring the jury to be from the state and district where the crime was committed. All of these provisions were calculated for the protection of the accused. The institution of the jury trial was highly regarded by the colonists: their experience with the bias of judges warranted their securing the right to a jury trial to all. Without the restriction as to the place of trial, the government could, if it wished to, remove the trial to a place far from the residence of the defendant, and make it impossible for him to adequately protect his interests. Even in this day of easy communication and travel, this requirement is sensible and valid.

Several other important rights were guaranteed by the Sixth Amendment. The accused has the right to be informed of the nature and cause of the accusation. In colonial times, the accused was not always fully informed as to the exact nature of the offense with which he was charged. This was done deliberately, in order that he might not be prepared to counter the testimony which was produced at the trial. Today it is perhaps even more important that the accused be informed of the "nature and cause of the accusation." The range of Federal crimes is considerably broader than it was in 1789: many of the new ones arise from complicated transactions, and minute specification of the charges are essential, if the accused is to know against what he must defend.

The matter of witnesses is dealt with in the Sixth Amendment. The accused has the right to see and hear the witnesses against him: he has the right to examine them. These rights are vital to the accused. Witnesses quite naturally tend to recount their testimony in a light favorable to the side which calls them: they may neglect to recount events which put a different light on the circumstances of the case. Unless the accused has the opportunity to see and hear them, and to question them concerning events, they may unwittingly give a distorted picture. There is the additional psychological factor that witnesses often tend to dramatize themselves: this tendency is diminished when they know that their testimony will be scrutinized for any exaggeration or misstatement. Not only has the accused the right of confrontation of witnesses adverse to himself, but he is guaranteed the right to enforce the presence of witnesses in his own behalf. This is a very powerful weapon in the arsenal of defense: without it the accused would frequently be unable to obtain the testimony of persons favorable to his cause, but reluctant to go to court. This guarantee puts him in the same position as the prosecution with respect to witnesses, and provides him the protection he must have.

The final right guaranteed by the Sixth Amendment is the right to counsel. Without this right, the accused would be faced by skillful and adroit counsel for the prosecution, unable to make a proper defense. But the importance of this right to representation extends back of the trial, and covers stages of procedure which are equally important to the defendant. He is entitled to be represented at the arraignment, the first step in the proceedings after arrest.

It is in the preliminary stages that the accused perhaps needs advice and counsel the most, since he may inadvertantly allow himself to be placed in such a position that at the time of trial his defense may be endangered.

Amendment VIII serves as a protection of the accused at two stages of the proceedings against him. The first restriction upon the government and the court is the amount of bail which may be fixed. To allow the court to set excessive bail would be, in most cases, to condemn the accused to jail before his guilt was established. Unable to raise the bail, he would have to remain in custody until trial. When this possibility is coupled with unwarranted delay in bringing the case to trial, the wisdom of the amendments dealing with these matters is clear. Similarly the restriction against excessive fines is wise, since the convicted person must pay the fine assessed before he may be released. Inability to pay an excessive fine would in effect subject him to an imprisonment to which he had not been sentenced. Cruel and unusual punishments are also forbidden. The eighteenth century was not noted for its mercy, and branding, slitting of ears and other cruel punishments were fresh in the minds of the colonists at the time of the Revolution.

One right was embedded in the original constitution. This was the provision in Article III, Section 9, that the privilege of the writ of habeas corpus should not be suspended, except in times of rebellion or invasion, when the public safety might require it. The writ of habeas corpus is an order, issued by a court, requiring the person to whom it is directed to produce the body of a person in his custody before that court, for the purpose of determining whether the detention is lawful. The writ was developed in England to check illegal imprisonments, and the colonists had had enough experience with unlawful detentions to demand that the right to this writ should not be suspended. It is important that the right to this writ be preserved, since it is frequently the only way of reviewing the procedures leading up to the detention as well as the lawfulness of the detention itself. Over-zealous police at times violate the right of a person to a prompt arraignment, keeping him in detention while they attempt to obtain sufficient evidence to make an actual charge against him. The person is being unlawfully detained, and the writ of habeas corpus forces the police to produce him in court, for the determination of the legality of their actions. Although the writ is most frequently used in criminal cases, it has its place in civil actions as well, as in cases involving the custody of children.

Civil Rights Under the Fourteenth Amendment

Perhaps the most far-reaching amendment of the Federal Constitution with respect to civil rights is Section One of the Fourteenth Amendment:

> All persons born or naturalized in the United States, and subject to the jurisdiction thereof, are citizens of the United States and of the State wherein they reside. No State shall make or enforce any law which shall abridge the privileges and immunities of citizens of the United States; nor shall any State deprive any person of life, liberty, or property, without due process of law; nor deny to any person within its jurisdiction the equal protection of the laws.

Proposed to the legislatures of the states in 1866, it was declared in force July 26, 1868.

The United States was faced with an acute situation immediately after the Civil War, heightened by the nature of the conflict. The Fourteenth Amendment was adopted to prevent discrimination against the Negroes by state action, which was clearly foreseeable. In certain areas of the country this mandate was sought to be avoided by means of segregation: states made mandatory separate facilities and accommodations for the different races, in schools, public buildings, public transportation. The matter of separate facilities as meeting the requirement of equal protection of the law was considered in the Supreme Court in the case of *Plessy* v. *Ferguson*, 163 U. S. 537 (1896), involving separate seating in railroad coaches. In that case the Supreme Court held that the constitutional requirement of equal protection was satisfied when the races are supplied substantially equal facilities, even though they are separate.

The judicial interpretation of the phrase "equal protection" underwent considerable change in the late 1940's and 1950's. In a number of cases decided in that period, the Supreme Court held that at the graduate school level, white students enjoyed benefits not shared by Negroes of similar educational qualifications in segregated schools, and ordered that Negroes be admitted to the professional schools formerly open only to white students. In 1954 the Supreme Court decided in *Brown* v. *Board of Education of Topeka, Kansas,* 347 U. S. 483, that:

> "in the field of public education the doctrine of 'separate but equal' has no place. Separate educational facilities are inherently unequal. Therefore, we hold that the plaintiffs and others similarly situated for whom the actions have been brought are, by reason of the segregation complained of, deprived of the equal protection of the laws guaranteed by the Fourteenth Amendment."

Since that decision, despite resistance in the hard-core states of the Deep South, desegregation has proceeded gradually in the public schools of eight states previously enforcing segregation.

The Court had held previously in *Shelley* v. *Kraemer,* 334 U. S. 1 (1948) that restrictive covenants directed against the sale of property to Negroes could not be enforced in state courts, since the exercise of the judicial process in enforcing such discriminatory deeds was state action under the terms of the Fourteenth Amendment, and was therefore unconstitutional. In 1956, the Court, without opinion, held that a city ordinance, segregating Negroes on city buses, was a violation of the "equal protection" clause. Thus the interpretation of the "equal protection" clause has broadened, and the violations of the Fourteenth Amendment on the part of the states and their agents—the judiciary, the legislature and municipalities—are being eliminated. In the period since 1945, in particular, substantial progress, through law, has been made in eliminating discrimination and segregation in employment, education, housing, public accommodations and social welfare. While these practices are not totally a thing of the past, both government and informed public opinion, in the majority of instances, are allied in the cause of equal rights regardless of race, color or creed.

In considering the abolition of segregation in the United States, several factors must be borne in mind. One is the division of powers between the states and the United States; the Congress and the Federal judiciary are specifically limited in their spheres of activity. In addition, a decision by the Supreme Court that a particular course of conduct is unconstitutional cannot, under our form of government, carry with it a decree which would be enforcible against everyone. The courts decide individual cases, based on particular facts and involving a limited number of persons as parties to the suit. While the decision in one case would control in other similar cases, each can deal only with the parties involved. Thus enforcement becomes a lengthy and piecemeal process, as the court decision must then be applied locally. A third factor, which is of the utmost importance, is the human one. Social prejudices cannot be overcome alone by legislation or court fiat.

In other areas the Supreme Court has had the meaning and application of the Fourteenth Amendment before it, and has by its decision extended the Federal Bill of Rights to cover other state actions. As was said by Mr. Justice Cardozo, in *Palko* v. *State of Connecticut*, 302 U. S. 319, 325 (1937):

"immunities that are valid as against the federal government by force of the specific pledges of particular amendments have been found to be implicit in the concept of ordered liberty, and thus, through the Fourteenth Amendment, become valid as against the states."

He cited as examples freedom of speech and of the press, the free exercise of religion, the right of peaceable assembly, and the right of one accused of crime to benefit of counsel. On the other hand, the Supreme Court has held that trial by jury may be modified or abolished by a state without being inconsistent with the Fourteenth Amendment. The line between those portions of the Bill of Rights which are extended by the Fourteenth Amendment and those which are not is admittedly not easy to draw. Mr. Justice Cardozo phrased the distinction in this manner:

"The right to trial by jury and the immunity from prosecution except as the result of an indictment may have value and importance. Even so, they are not of the very essence of a scheme of ordered liberty. To abolish them is not to violate a 'principle of justice so rooted in the traditions and conscience of our people as to be ranked as fundamental.' . . .

"We reach a different plane of social and moral values when we pass to the privileges and immunities that have been taken over from the earlier articles of the federal bill of rights and brought within the Fourteenth Amendment by a process of absorption. These in their origin were effective against the federal government alone. If the Fourteenth Amendment has absorbed them, the process of absorption has had its source in the belief that neither liberty nor justice would exist if they were sacrificed."

Just what these privileges and immunities are depends on judicial interpretation.

Judicial Interpretation

The constitutions of the states and of the United States are almost identical, insofar as provisions for freedoms and liberties are concerned, as indicated on the accompanying chart. However, there is considerable variation among the states and the Federal courts with respect to what actions are considered violative of the same provision of their constitutions, couched in identical language.

The constitutions of both Pennsylvania and Oklahoma provide that no accused may be compelled to give evidence against himself. The Pennsylvania Supreme Court has held that evidence of contraband liquor found under an improperly issued search warrant will not be suppressed, as violating this particular provision of the Pennsylvania constitution. The Oklahoma Supreme Court has reached the opposite conclusion, and has suppressed such illegally-obtained evidence. The explanation for this divergence of views is that there is no magic in words themselves, no exact meaning to be ascribed to a phrase. Courts will vary in their interpretation of what is meant by certain language, just as will ordinary citizens. They may all agree that certain acts within a narrow range are violative of a particular provision, but they may very well differ as to what other acts come within the protection of the constitution. There need be no uniformity under our legal system, since the state supreme courts are the final arbiters of the meaning of the provisions of their own constitutions.

The Supreme Court of the United States is without power to correct decisions of a state supreme court respecting the state constitution, even though it would decide the case differently. The only time it overrules the decision of a state court is when a Federal question is involved. A decision by the Supreme Court of the United States in such a case clearly requires that the state courts follow that decision, but only because a Federal question is involved.

SELECTED READINGS

For other materials, see Bibliography, page 121.

Carr, Robert Kenneth. Federal protection of civil rights. Ithaca, Cornell university press, 1947.

Cushman, Robert, Eugene. Civil liberties in the United States. Ithaca, Cornell university press, 1956.

Dumbauld, Edward. The Bill of Rights and what it means today. Norman, University of Oklahoma press, 1957.

Newman, Edwin S. The law of civil rights and civil liberties. New York, Oceana publications, 1957.

Chapter 3

STATE COURTS, THEIR JURISDICTION AND ORGANIZATION

Jurisdiction

The creation of a court or a system of courts immediately poses the problem of jurisdiction. Jurisdiction may be broadly defined as the right and power of a court to determine the issues which are presented to it, and to enforce its decrees and judgments. To some, concern over a court's jurisdiction may seem to be legalistic maneuvering to confuse and delay the course of justice. Actually, jurisdiction is the most important element in our court system. Without this element, an orderly system would turn into chaos and, even more important, rights of citizens might be violated, if not destroyed.

When a court is established, either by constitution or by statute, it is given certain functions to perform and certain powers to enable it to do so. Whether these be broad or narrow, the court can operate only within their limitations —this is its jurisdiction. For a court to act beyond its powers would be usurpation of authority; the court would be acting in a non-lawful manner. When jurisdiction is considered as a limitation upon the authority, and a definition of the power, of a court to act, emphasis upon it ceases to be a clouding of the issues, and becomes instead the establishment of the fundamental fact of the court's very right to act in a particular case.

The jurisdiction of a court, whether established by constitution or by legislation is always limited. Even the Supreme Court of the United States does not have unlimited jurisdiction; it cannot do certain things which are in the power of other Federal courts. The highest courts of the states are similarly limited. Likewise, courts of original jurisdiction, those in which suits must be commenced, where the case is tried, witnesses testify and judgment is entered, have their own jurisdictional limitations.

Courts of orginal jurisdiction in the state systems are frequently divided by the types of cases they may hear. The most usual division is between civil and criminal matters, and separate courts deal only with their appropriate kinds of cases. In some states such a division is unnecessary, but in the most populous states this simple division is found insufficient. In these it has been found necessary to have a number of different civil and criminal courts. The ordinary limitation in civil matters is a monetary one; the amount of money involved determines the court which has jurisdiction. Similarly criminal courts have their limitations with respect to the seriousness of the offense charged.

There are other means of limiting jurisdiction in civil courts. Some courts are not given the power to determine the ownership of real estate, although they may deal with claims for rent. A few states still preserve the distinction between actions at law and proceedings in equity, and provide distinct courts for the trial of these two different types of civil actions.

So far jurisdiction has been considered as a definition of scope of a court's authority to hear and determine cases. But the word has another important meaning. A court must also have jurisdiction, i.e. control, over the persons or things involved; it must be able to enforce its judgment properly. Ordinarily a defendant in a civil suit must be served with a summons from the court, in order that the court can hear and finally determine the matter. Otherwise suit might be brought and judgment entered by the court without notice to the defendant, who would be personally bound by the result. But once such a summons has been properly served, the defendant cannot evade judgment by refusal to appear in answer to the summons. In most states the summons of a court is effective only within the county or judicial district for which the court is established. Hence suit must be brought in the judicial district where the defendant lives or where he may be found for service of that court's process.

And in no case can the process of a state court extend beyond the state line.

In certain instances personal service of a summons may be unnecessary if the object of the suit is to affect a "res" or "thing" which is within the jurisdiction of the court. If this were not the case, many claims to such "things" as real estate could not be settled so long as a claimant kept beyond the jurisdiction of the court where the property was located. Thus, in these instances, the location of the property rather than of the individual becomes the test of jurisdiction.

Organization

There is no uniformity in the organization of the various state court systems. Each state has had to develop its own to fit its particular needs. However, there is a common pattern of rank, for both civil and criminal courts. This gradation serves two purposes: one is the division of jurisdiction among two or more courts, according to the seriousness of the offense or the monetary value of the claim involved; the other, and by far the more important to the citizens of the states, is to provide a method of review by a higher and impartial court. Perhaps there is no feature of our court systems which affords greater protection than this right of review. Whether the review consists of an actual new trial of the case by the appellate court, as occasionally happens, or simply a review of the original proceedings, the assurance of this right is a precious one.

Every state court system provides for some kind of minor judiciary of limited jurisdiction for the trial of small claims or petty criminal offenses. The most familiar one is the justice of the peace, alderman or magistrate. The justice of the peace historically handled only criminal cases, as the title indicates, but in this country he also takes care of small civil claims. In cities, the equivalent may be an elected official, called magistrate or alderman. This minor judiciary, which affords quick and easy access to the judicial process, is one of the real merits of the legal systems of all of our states.

In some of the larger cities, special courts have been set up with more expansive jurisdiction than the justice of the

peace or the magistrate, but with the same advantages of
speed and informality. No decision of these minor courts is
final; an appeal can always be taken to a higher court. The
court to which such appeals go is generally the more formal
general trial court which has no generic name and can be
called, for convenience, the district court.

The district court is the court of the jury trial. It hears
originally civil cases which involve amounts or matters beyond the jurisdiction of the minor courts, and criminal cases
which the minor courts are not empowered to hear. Also,
it often acts as the court which reviews the decision of the
minor judiciary. These courts are conducted in a formal
manner and the services of an attorney, while not required,
are generally regarded as essential.

The decision in any case tried in these district courts may
be appealed to an appellate court. The number and rank
of these courts depend on the size of the state and the
amount of litigation which goes on, and their jurisdiction
varies accordingly. Some states have two appellate courts,
one an intermediate court with jurisdiction limited to special types of cases or to those involving limited amounts of
money or the less serious crimes; the other, the highest court
in the state which has unlimited jurisdiction. It is not always possible for the angry citizen to do as he threatens;
he may not be able to take his case "right up to the Supreme
Court", but he always does have the right to have the
decision of the original trial court reviewed by an appellate court of some type.

In a court which hears only appeals, the cases are not
tried over again. The judges of the appellate court have
before them the record of the proceedings in the trial court.
The appellate court examines this record, and if it finds that
there has been an error committed which prejudices the
appellant, it orders appropriate relief. If one had to select
the feature of our court system which gives the greatest
protection to the rights of all concerned, the right to a review by a higher court might well be that feature.

Criminal Law

Broadly speaking, criminal law is that branch of law which treats of crimes and their punishment. It includes the investigation of crimes, the kinds and nature of evidence which must be produced at a trial, and the circumstances which may relieve one from criminal liability.

Criminal courts deal with the trial of cases arising from criminal offenses, which are divided into two kinds: misdemeanor is an offense which is considered to be minor and is usually limited in punishment to a relatively small fine or short imprisonment or both. A felony is one which is made serious by reason of the elements which it includes, and carries heavier punishment. Exceeding the speed limit is a misdemeanor. In and of itself it is simply an infraction of the rules of safety of the road, even though it might at times contribute to something more serious. Burglary, on the other hand, is a felony, even though the burglar takes nothing, because of the serious nature of the elements which are included, that is, breaking and entering the household of another in the night time with intent to steal. This classification of crimes is important because it often determines the court which hears the case and may affect the formalities of procedure, not to mention the severity of sentence.

Presumption of Innocence

Regardless of whether one is accused of the most innocuous of misdemeanors or the most serious of felonies, under our system of criminal law he has the benefit of one principle in the proceedings involving him which is of incalculable value. In this country a person is presumed to be innocent until proved guilty. This is important, because it makes it necessary for the prosecution to prove guilt beyond a reasonable doubt. This may appear to be an undeserved advantage to the guilty. And so it is, but what of the innocent person who has been accused of a crime? Clearly there cannot be two rules, one for the innocent and a different one for the guilty, since the determination of which rule to apply would necessitate the actual decision of guilt or innocence. Therefore, the rule of presumption of innocence is always applied. An analogous concept which guides our criminal law is that it is better that 99 guilty persons should escape punishment than that one innocent person should suffer. Miscarriages of justice are bound to occur in any system which man can devise. Innocent persons have been convicted, even in a system operating under this principle, but it is certainly clear that in such a system there will be fewer such mistakes. The innocent must be protected to the utmost, even though this means that some of the guilty escape punishment.

Place of Trial

Another general principle of the criminal law is that the trial must take place in the judicial district in which the crime occurred. This rule goes back historically to the time when the jury began to function. Since the jurymen were supposed to be familiar with the events and to weigh the testimony of the witnesses against their own knowledge, it was necessary that the trial take place where the crime had been committed. This rule of procedure is for the protection of the defendant. If it were not for this requirement, a state might use its resources to remove a trial to a distant county, to the detriment of the defense of the accused. Moreover it is an entirely reasonable rule, since the witnesses are most likely to be residents of the county where the crime was committed. However, by statute in some states, the court is given authority to grant a "change of venue", that is, order that the trial take place in another judicial district, if it believes that the atmosphere of the community is such that a fair and impartial trial cannot be had.

Criminal Courts

The criminal law is administered by the state courts at varying levels in much the same manner as is the civil law. At the lowest level, we have the minor judiciary (the justice of the peace, the magistrate or alderman), whose functions in the criminal law field differ somewhat from those which they exercise in civil matters. Above them are the general criminal trial courts, which correspond to the civil courts of general jurisdiction, and in which the jury trials are held. Appeals from these trial courts may go to a special criminal appeals court or to the general appellate courts which also hear civil appeals. There are variations within a state and between states to the same degree as in the civil courts.

Initial Procedure

Criminal cases ordinarily begin in one of two ways. A police officer makes an arrest without a warrant, or the arrest is made on a warrant issued by a magistrate. The warrant is issued upon the complaint of a private citizen or at the request of the police after the investigation of a crime. In order that the accused may not be deprived of the right of due process of law, he must be taken before one of the minor judiciary without delay for a hearing.

The minor judiciary or the magistrate, a more familiar name, goes far back into English legal history. He functions in every state. In rural areas, he is usually the justice of the peace, while in the city he may be called a police magistrate or alderman. His jurisdiction to hear and decide cases, and perform other functions, is set out in the state statutes. He acts in two capacities, depending on the seriousness of the offense charged. He acts as a trial court in cases involving misdemeanors which are punishable by a small fine or a short jail sentence, this jurisdiction varying from state to state. In all other cases he acts only as a committing magistrate; his decision is not the final disposition of the case.

At the hearing or arraignment before the magistrate, the testimony of the complainant and others called by him is heard. The person charged must be present and have an opportunity to cross-examine the witnesses against him. He may, if he chooses, make a statement or present his side of the case. If the offense is a minor one, as to which the magistrate has the right to find the accused guilty or not guilty, the magistrate decides the matter at the conclusion of the hearing. If he finds the accused not guilty, the latter is discharged and the case is ended. If the accused is found guilty, he is immediately fined or sentenced to jail. If he is found guilty, he may appeal to the higher court which has jurisdiction to hear such appeals. In this appeal court, the case is usually tried anew and is not heard as an ordinary appeal.

If the case involves the kind of offense over which the magistrate has no final jurisdiction, the effect of the hearing is different. In such cases the committing magistrate only determines whether, on the testimony presented before him, there is sufficient evidence to justify holding the accused for trial by the proper court. The accused has the same rights as in the other type of hearing, but frequently he does not present any evidence in his defense. He may even waive the hearing, since he will have an opportunity to present his case in the trial court. If the committing magistrate does not believe that there is sufficient evidence produced, he dismisses the complaint and discharges the accused. If, however, he feels that there is sufficient evidence, he "holds" the accused for court. He must set bail at a reasonable amount, except for capital offenses. If the accused can produce the bail required, he is at liberty until he is required to appear for trial. Failing to supply bail, he is remanded to jail to await trial.

Grand Jury

There is an intervening step between the preliminary hearing and the actual trial in most states. This is action by the grand jury. The committing magistrate forwards to the clerk of the trial court a copy of the record of the case. On the basis of this record a bill of indictment is drawn up by the prosecuting attorney's office. The bill specifies the details of the crime, as to place, date and person, and the specific crime or crimes.

In presenting the case before the grand jury, the prosecuting attorney delivers the bill of indictment to the grand jury and then presents the testimony of witnesses to substantiate the indictment. The accused is not present at the grand jury hearing nor may he be represented by counsel. The proceedings before the grand jury are secret, so far as the testimony is concerned,, but this cannot harm the accused. If he is indicted, he will be made aware of the exact nature of the crime charged, and in many states the names of the witnesses who appeared before the grand jury are written on the indictment. Thus the accused knows who testified, even though he is unaware of what the witnesses said. In any event he will have his day in court, because the grand jury indictment is not a conviction. If the grand jury does not believe that the state has produced sufficient evidence to justify trial of the accused for the crime charged, it "ignores" the bill, that is, it refuses to indict. If it believes that a sufficient case has been made out, it returns a "true bill", that is, it expresses its belief that the bill of indictment is correct and that the accused should be tried. This is merely a confirmation of the action of the committing magistrate.

Grand jury proceedings have been criticized because they are a repetition of the preliminary hearing with attendant inconvenience to witnesses. But it may be that the committing magistrate held a person for court on too little evidence. In such a case, the grand jury, by refusing to indict, relieves both the prosecution and the accused of the necessity of going to trial. If it is not satisfied with the evidence produced only by the prosecution, it is unlikely that a regular jury would convict after hearing both sides. Moreover, the grand jury is an investigating body. Frequently it exercises its rights to investigate matters which come to its attention, with the result that it may on its own motion indict persons whom it determines to be violators of the law.

The Criminal Trial

After an indictment is returned, the case goes on the trial list of the criminal court. In its turn the case is reached. Here the prosecution must prove its case beyond a reasonable doubt in view of all the evidence. Here again the defendant must be present and he has the right to representation by counsel and the right to cross-examine the witnesses for the prosecution. He has the right to compel the attendance of witnesses on his own behalf. The prosecution may not call him as a witness, since the state constitutions provide that no one in a criminal case can be compelled to be a witness against himself. The jury cannot draw any inference from his failure to take the stand; otherwise the constitutional privilege against self-incrimination would be meaningless, since the natural inference would be that if he were to testify truthfully his testimony would support the case of the prosecution.

The trial of a criminal case generally follows the procedure of a civil trial. Perhaps there are more histrionics in the addresses of the prosecutor and counsel for the defense, a greater appeal to the emotions, than in civil cases. But the safeguards of individual rights are zealously observed. The courts are very careful to examine any claim that constitutional rights have been infringed. These rights are just as important as they were in 1776. Unfortunately overzealous police and prosecuting attorneys sometimes violate them, and it is the function of the courts to see to it that these errors are corrected.

Appeal

If the verdict is "not guilty", the case is at an end. However, if the defendant is found guilty, he may take an appeal to the appropriate appellate court. The prosecution in criminal cases cannot ordinarily take an appeal, because if it were successful, the defendant would be tried a second time for the same offense, in violation of constitutional provisions. This restriction against a second trial for the same offense does not apply in the case of a new trial granted upon the appeal of the defendant. By taking an appeal he waives his constitutional protection, since it is to his advantage to do so.

Many of us are familiar with criminal cases which have been tried and appealed three or four times. To the laymen these repeated trials and appeals seem almost a travesty of justice, but that is not the case. We must remember that all cases are tried under specific rules, and these rules must be followed. A case is not sent back for a new trial by an appellate court unless it finds a violation of one of these rules which has prevented the defendant from receiving the kind of trial to which he is entitled. Perhaps the guilty do escape on so-called technicalities, or because witnesses have either disappeared or become so hazy in their recollection as not to be convincing. But we must remember that under our system a man is innocent until he is proved guilty beyond a reasonable doubt, and in a fair and impartial trial.

Bail

What has been said with respect to granting bail prior to the trial of a case also applies while an appeal is pending. Laymen may wonder why someone who has been found guilty of a crime by a jury should be allowed to walk the streets, a relatively free man. The theory that a man is not guilty until he has been so proved includes the total course of the proceeding through the appellate courts. Until the appellate court finally decides the case, he must be considered in the same light as he was during the period between the original hearing and his trial in the district court. Everyone has read stories of men who have been arrested for a crime, set free on bail, and then arrested for a subsequent crime. The reaction of many is that his freedom on bail is an abuse of the privilege. Why should a criminal be allowed at large, thus able to commit other crimes; why should he not be in jail? The answer is again the same; we must not confuse arrest or indictment or even conviction by a jury as synonymous with guilt. Guilt should not attach until there is a *final* decision. Until that time, the defendant must be allowed his freedom on bail. The fact that he is arrested for an offense alleged to have been committed while free on bail does not change the situation. The fact may be that, had he not been arrested for the first crime, he might not have been arrested for the second.

The workings of justice become more understandable when we look at the other side of the coin. People have been arrested and convicted for crimes which they did not commit. Would any of us feel that these guiltless persons should be denied bail, either before trial or pending an appeal? Obviously the answer would be "no." In order to protect the innocent, we must extend the privileges of bail to everyone, until the case has been finally decided.

Sentence

When the final determination of guilt is made in a criminal case, there remains the problem of the sentence to be imposed. It is the duty of the court which tried the case to fix the sentence. A penalty is provided for each crime, and this may be a fine, imprisonment. or both. In most instances this penalty is not fixed, but has minimum and maximum limits. It is up to the court to determine what the penalty shall be, within those limits. This is one of the most difficult tasks which a judge has to perform. He must balance the interests of society and the individual. What sentence is best, under all the circumstances of the case? In order to reach his decision, the judge often has recourse to the defendant's family, neighbors and friends, social workers and any others who can assist him in making this important decision.

During the past 150 years we have changed our views with respect to the penalty for the commission of a crime. It is safe to say that in 1800 punishment was the main purpose of the penalty. Today the emphasis is not upon punishment or retribution, but upon rehabilitation. Probation, parole and the suspended sentence are all evidences of this. Progress along these lines is slow to be sure. Perfection is far from being attained, but crime and punishment are now recognized as social problems. Juvenile courts, youth study centers, psychiatry, mental health clinics and other innovations are signs of the change in viewpoint and of an enlightened effort to get at the sources of trouble and correct them.

Civil Courts

While the civil courts are not as widely publicized nor as well known as the criminal courts, they are of equal importance. Instead of affecting the life or liberty of the citizen, they deal with property rights. They are organized along lines similar to the criminal courts, and frequently the same court deals with both types of cases.

Minor Judiciary

Every state provides for at least one court to handle small civil claims. The jurisdiction of these courts is limited in amount, as well as in kinds of cases. The main purpose of these courts is to provide a means of settling small claims quickly. One of their virtues is the informality which prevails. In most instances the contestants are not represented by counsel; the amounts in controversy are so small that the employment of counsel would result in a loss to the claimant. Not infrequently the magistrate effects some kind of settlement, saving the parties the inevitable bitterness of a public trial. Since the magistrate is a local person, his advice is frequently sought and his influence in the neighborhood is considerable. It is well that we do have these courts to try claims which, though small in amount, loom large in the lives of the parties.

Ordinarily in such courts the plaintiff need not file any formal declaration of his claim; he merely notifies the clerk of the amount and nature of his claim, a summons is issued, and a time for a hearing is set. At the hearing, the proceedings are very simple. The plaintiff and his witnesses testify, and the defendant has the right to examine them. Then the defendant and his witnesses tell their story, again with the right to examination by the opposite party. At the conclusion of the testimony, the magistrate gives judgment. Either party may appeal the decision to a higher court, usually the civil jury trial court.

The defendant, of course, may choose to pay, if the decision is against him. He may refuse to pay, or may be unable to make payment. In such a case the plaintiff takes steps to collect his judgment, by means of the magistrate's officer. The latter is instructed as to where he may find goods of the defendant. He then proceeds to "levy" on them, that is, he takes possession of them in the name of the court, and notifies the defendant that they will be sold to satisfy the claim of the plaintiff. The defendant is not permitted to remove the goods or to sell them, since they are now in the possession of the court. At the time appointed for the sale, the magistrate's officer sells the goods at auction to the highest bidder, and the proceeds, after payment of the costs of the case, go to the plaintiff, up to the amount of his judgment. Only enough of the defendant's goods are sold to recover the amount due the plaintiff and the costs of the suit.

District Courts

The bulk of civil trials take place in the district courts, which have the most inclusive jurisdiction in the state systems. In the district courts we meet not only the complicated rules of evidence, but the formalities of pleading, that is, the formal written statements of the complaint of the plaintiff and the answer of the defendant, as well as other supplementary papers which may be involved.

Most cases are tried before a jury, although both sides may agree to a trial without a jury. The selection of the jury in a civil case follows the pattern of the criminal courts, but ordinarily counsel do not make as much of the selection of the jury as they do in criminal cases. Most civil cases have had little or no newspaper publicity, and prospective jurors are less likely to have any prejudices about the case. Following the selection of the jury, the case proceeds in much the same manner as a criminal case: examination and cross-examination of witnesses, the addresses to the jury, the charge of the court, and the deliberations and verdict of the jury.

The side which has lost in the trial court may wish to ask for a new trial or for a complete reversal of the verdict reached in the trial court. The nominal winner may be dissatisfied with the rulings or the amount or character of the verdict of the jury. Therefore either side may appeal, and in many instances both sides do so. Appeals are heard in the appropriate appellate court of the state, in the same manner as appeals in criminal cases. The court which hears these appeals is specified by statute; it may be an intermediate court, because of the amount or character of claim, or it may be the highest court of appeal. Here again state law determines the course of an appeal.

Non-Jury Trial Courts

When constitutional guarantees were discussed, mention was made of jury trials in "suits at common law". Originally the common law courts, where the jury trials were had, were the only ones in England. However, they had their shortcomings; they were devoted to form and were not responsive to the needs of the people. Appeals for redress of grievances, for which the common law courts gave no relief, were addressed to the king, who turned them over to his chancellor for action. In time this function of the chancellor became so onerous that he established a court, known as the court of chancery or court of equity, to hear such cases. It was in these courts that people sought relief which the common law courts could not furnish. For example, only the court of chancery was able to issue an injunction to prevent the performance of an act which might cause irreparable harm to the plaintiff. Since the granting of redress was within the discretion of the chancellor or judge, no juries were ever involved. Thus when the colonists made provision for jury trials, they were aware of this aspect of equity jurisdiction, and their constitutions simply provide for jury trials in such actions as had required them before the Revolution.

Another court which has never had a jury as a regular part of its procedure is that which deals with the affairs of a deceased person. Originally the ecclesiastical courts handled such matters, but eventually this function was taken over in England by the chancellor's court. In the colonies, separate courts were usually set up, and for the most part a separate system of courts for the handling of decedents' estates exists in the states today. The constitutional provisions with respect to jury trials do not include this kind of court, known as the probate or surrogate's court. Appeals from both the court of equity and the probate court follow the same system as do other civil actions.

Enforcement of Judgments

It is not enough for a plaintiff to recover a judgment against the defendant; he must also be able to collect, or his suit is worthless. The general trial courts have all the powers of the magistrate's court to collect from the defendant, and others as well. The most powerful additional weapon is the power to sell the real estate of the defendant. The sheriff, under the proper authorization, "levies" on the real property, and after proper notice, sells it at public sale. This is a drastic method, and the ordinary defendant usually finds some means of paying judgment, rather than sacrifice his property. The sheriff, if given proper instructions, is also able to "levy" on such things as shares of stock and bank accounts, and to convert the interest of the defendant into money for the benefit of the plaintiff. The courts are equipped to collect the judgment for the plaintiff, if the defendant has the resources, but it does not do so on its own. It is up to the plaintiff to give the necessary instructions by means of specified procedures, in order to set the court's machinery in motion.

SELECTED READINGS

For other materials, see Bibliography, page 121.

Blume, William Wirt. American civil procedure. Englewood Cliff, N. J., Prentice-Hall, 1955.

Callender, Clarence N. American courts; their organization and procedure. New York, McGraw-Hill, 1927.

Mayers, Lewis. The American legal system. New York, Harpers, 1955.

Orfield, Lester Bernhardt. Criminal procedure from arrest to appeal. New York, New York univesity press, 1947.

Pound, Roscoe. Organization of courts. Boston, Little Brown, 1940.

Chapter 4

THE FEDERAL COURTS

As would be expected, the Federal system of courts follows the pattern set by the states. The Constitution provides for only one court by name, but authorizes the Congress to establish such others as it sees fit. At present there are two other courts, in addition to the Supreme Court of the United States, which are usually thought of as constituting the Federal court system. These are the District Court and the Court of Appeals.

The District Courts are the courts of original jurisdiction. They correspond to the general trial courts of the state systems. The country has been divided into more than 80 districts, each with its own District Court. The size of the district depends upon population and the amount of business coming before the court. Although no district is larger than a single state, some states may be divided into as many as four districts. The number of judges in each District Court is determined by the need of the particular court.

Above these courts are the Courts of Appeals for the eleven circuits into which the country is divided. These courts review the decisions of the District Courts within their respective circuits, as well as the decisions of some of the Federal administrative agencies. The highest court in the Federal system is, of course, the Supreme Court.

The District Courts are governed by the provisions of the Constitution, Federal laws and rules established by the Supreme Court. They deal with both civil and criminal matters. The right to a jury trial in all criminal cases is guaranteed by the Constitution, and is provided for in "suits at common law", that is, in cases in which jury trials were had in England before the Revolution. The rules of procedure differ in details from those of state courts, but the general pattern is the same. A trial in a District Court is almost indistinguishable from one in a state court. Of course the jurors are drawn from the wider area of the district, but they are still just a cross-section of a larger community.

The right to a review of the trial court's decision has been underscored as a great advantage of the state court system. The same right is enjoyed by the citizen whose case is tried in the Federal courts. No decision of a District Court is final; all are subject to review by the appropriate Court of Appeals. Although the rules with respect to review by the Supreme Court do not guarantee that every case can be taken before that court, this situation does not differ from that in many of the states with an intermediate court of appeal. It is the right to a review of the trial court's actions by an impartial and independent court, regardless of the rank of the reviewing court, which is important.

Jurisdiction of the Federal Courts

The judicial powers of the Federal courts are defined in section 2 of Article III of the Constitution:

"The judicial Power shall extend to all Cases, in Law and Equity, arising under this Constitution, the Laws of the United States, and Treaties made, or which shall be made, under their Authority;—to all Cases affecting Ambassadors, other public Ministers and Consuls:—to Controversies between two or more States:—between a State and Citizens of another State:—between Citizens of different States:—between Citizens of the same State claiming Lands under Grants of different States: —and between a State, or the Citizens thereof, and foreign States, Citizens or Subjects. In all cases affecting Ambassadors, other public Ministers and Consuls, the Supreme Court shall have original jurisdiction. In all the other cases before mentioned the Supreme Court shall have appellate jurisdiction both as to law and fact, with such exceptions and under such regulations as the Congress shall make."

These constitutional powers cannot be enlarged, except by amendment to the Constitution, but they may be limited. For instance, the judicial power of the United States extends to controversies between citizens of different states, but Congress has provided that the amount in controversy must exceed $3,000. Although the Supreme Court is granted original jurisdiction under the Constitution "in all cases affecting Ambassadors, other public Ministers and Consuls", Congress has decided that it is reasonable to subject consuls to the jurisdiction of the District Courts, as well as to that of the Supreme Court. Only the highest representative of a foreign state is now considered as having the right to have suits involving him instituted in the highest court of the land.

In large areas of the law, the jurisdiction of the state and Federal courts is "concurrent"; either has the power to hear and determine the issues of the particular case. The power of the state courts to hear and determine cases involving Federal law is implied in Article VI, Section 2 of the Constitution, which provides that the "Constitution and the Laws of the United States which shall be made in Pursuance thereof; and all Treaties made, or which shall be made, under the Authority of the United States, shall be the supreme Law of the Land, and the Judges in every State shall be bound thereby." However, Congress may reserve by legislation the exclusive right of the Federal courts to hear cases which arise under "the laws of the United States." Unless Congress so acts, the jurisdiction of the state and Federal courts is concurrent. The choice of forum is in the hands of the plaintiff, although the defendant may, where the circumstances permit, have the case removed from a state court to the appropriate Federal District Court.

As noted, the Congress has also seen fit to place another kind of limitation on civil matters which can be heard by the Federal Courts. Although the Constitution declares that the Federal courts shall exercise their judicial power in controversies "between citizens of different states", Congress has limited the jurisdiction of the District Courts in civil actions to those cases in which the matter in controversy exceeds the sum or value of $3,000. This limitation does not prevent a citizen of New Jersey from suing a citizen of Pennsylvania to recover a debt of $2,000. It merely means that the suit must be brought in a state court, instead of the

United States District Court. The same limitation of $3,000 applies to civil actions arising under the Constitution, laws or treaties of the United States: even though the law which gives rise to the rights and liabilities of the parties is Federal in source, a case involving these will not be heard by a Federal court if the amount involved is less than $3,000. Here again the parties are not deprived of any recourse to the courts; they are relegated to the appropriate state court to hear the action. There are certain kinds of cases arising under the Constitution or the laws of the United States which have no monetary limitation as to Federal court jurisdiction. Although such distinctions might appear to be capricious, they are in fact reasonable and often necessary. Without these limitations and restrictions, the Federal courts would be flooded with minor claims which can be as well tried in the state courts, and at less expense to the parties and the taxpayers.

Jurisdiction in Criminal Cases

There is no difficulty in understanding the jurisdiction of the Federal courts in criminal matters. They have exclusive jurisdiction in cases involving the violation of the criminal laws of the United States. At the outset there were only a few Federal crimes, such as theft of mail in the custody of the Post Office or smuggling. With the passage of time, enlarged activities of the Federal government and the development of interstate commerce increased the number of acts which have been designated as criminal by Congress. Many of them have to do with interstate transactions. The theft of an automobile is solely a matter of state concern, so long as the car remains inside the state. But when a stolen car is transported across a state line, it becomes a part of commerce between the states, subject to Federal control. Congress has made such an action a Federal crime. Wilful violations of many Federal regulatory laws, such as the Internal Revenue Act and the Bankruptcy Act, have been made crimes by Congress. Regardless of the nature of the offenses, Federal crimes can only be prosecuted in the Federal courts.

The constitutional guarantees of the Bill of Rights, such as the grand jury, the prompt trial, the right of confrontation of witnesses and the freedom from illegal searches and seizures, are scrupulously protected by the Federal courts. Only a few years ago a government secretary was arrested in New York in the act of passing stolen government documents to a foreign agent. There was clear and convincing proof that she had taken the documents from an office in Washington, and she had been observed handing them to the foreign agent. She was convicted in the Federal District Court, but the conviction was set aside by the Court of Appeals because the government's case was based on illegally obtained information, and other evidence otherwise unobtainable but for this illegal procedure. Government agents had tapped her telephone conversations in violation of Federal statutes and had thus learned of her activities. Acting on this information, they trailed her to New York and arrested her immediately after she had passed on the stolen documents. Evidence obtained by wire-tapping is inadmissible in the Federal courts. Moreover, the Circuit Court of Appeals held that evidence which could only have been developed from such illegally obtained evidence was likewise inadmissible. Since the government's entire case stemmed from the illegal wire-tapping, it had no evidence free of this taint to present in a second trial, and hence did not proceed.

This is an extreme illustration of the care with which the Federal courts scrutinize criminal proceedings to protect the constitutional rights of the defendants. It is this desire to protect the rights of the defendants which gives rise to the issuance of writs of habeas corpus by the Federal courts, after conviction and final appeal in the state courts. The purpose of these proceedings is not to examine the defendant's rights under the state laws, but to make sure that his Federal rights have not been violated.

The Supreme Court

The Supreme Court of the United States has the right to review the decisions of the lower Federal courts, subject to

certain limitations placed on it by Congress. One method
of review is by an appeal, which is a matter of right. An
appeal, in this technical sense, can only be taken in cases in
which a Circuit Court of Appeals has declared a state
statute to be invalid as being in contravention of the Constitution, treaties or laws of the United States. The other
method of review is by a petition for a writ of certiorari.
The granting of these petitions is a matter of discretion
with the Supreme Court, which denies a majority of them.
If the petition is granted, the records of the court below are
sent up to the Supreme Court for review.

To bring a case from the highest court of a state before
the Supreme Court is difficult. The Supreme Court does not
decide questions of state law; that is the function of the state
courts. An appeal, in the technical sense, can be taken from
the highest court of a state where the validity of a Federal
treaty or statute has been questioned and has been found
invalid by the state court, or where the validity of a state
statute has been questioned as repugnant to the Constitution or laws of the United States and the decision was in
favor of its validity. From this it will be seen that the
Supreme Court is not reviewing state law in such appeals,
but it is only considering the validity of statutes from the
Federal view. The Court will also, in its discretion, review
on certiorari judgments where the validity of a Federal
statute is drawn in question, or where the validity of a state
statute is questioned on the ground of its being repugnant
to the Constitution, treaties or laws of the United States.
Here again the heart of the matter is a Federal question,
and does not depend for its solution on the determination
of state law.

Procedure in the Supreme Court is similar to that in other
appellate courts—the filing of briefs, oral argument by counsel, the handing down of a written opinion. But by the very
nature of the Court, all aspects are touched with more for-
mality and decorum. The dignity and solemnity of the
court-room are in themselves a silent guarantee that the
questions presented to the Court will be determined according to the law of the land, as it is understood and inter-

preted by nine men who, by reason of the eminence of their position, are beyond the reach of any outside pressure.

Other Federal Courts

The court system of the United States is not limited to the courts which have been described. From time to time Congress has established special courts to handle particular kinds of litigation. The Court of Claims hears cases involving claims against the United States which, like other sovereigns, cannot be sued in the ordinary courts. This court is located in Washington and does not try cases elsewhere.

Appeals from the customs appraisers go to the Customs Court, and the Court of Customs and Patent Appeals reviews the decisions of the Customs Court and of the Patent Office and Tariff Commission. Perhaps the best known of these auxiliary courts is the Tax Court of the United States, formerly the Board of Tax Appeals, which hears appeals from the decisions of the Internal Revenue Service. The Emergency Court of Appeals was established during World War II to determine the validity of regulations issued under the Emergency Price Control Act of 1942, and was continued under the post-war price stabilization act.

One recently established court grew out of World War II. For a century and a half the rules governing military justice had been relatively unchanged. The vast influx of the youth of the country into the armed forces in the '40's, with the accompanying difficulties of adjustment to military discipline, brought about great dissatisfaction with the methods and rules of the system of military justice. As a result, the system was completely overhauled, and a new Code of Military Justice was enacted. Under the new code members of the armed forces have all the protections afforded the civilian by the Constitution. Enlisted personnel now have the right to request that other enlisted men be members of the court martial. The greatest change was in the establishment of the Court of Military Appeals. This court, composed of three civilians, is the highest reviewing body, and reviews all cases of military justice involving a general or a flag officer, or sentences of death. It may also review other cases upon petition of the accused, and cases forwarded by the Judge Advocate General. The importance of this court lies in the fact that there is now a final reviewing body which is outside the military forces, and which is not subject to the pressures which might conceivably arise in military channels. The Code of Military Justice is in many respects more modern and responsive to the needs of the day than many civil codes.

Taken as a whole, the judicial system of the United States, complicated though it must necessarily be in view of the size and complexity of the country, serves admirably to decide the controversies of its citizens. No one would claim perfection for it, but it is a live and constantly developing branch of our civilization. Improvement of the system and its administration is one of the functions of the lawyer and the Bar.

SELECTED READINGS

For further materials, see Bibliography, page 121.

Bunn, Charles Wilson. A brief survey of the jurisdiction and practice of the courts of the United States. St. Paul, West, 1949.

Frankfurter, Felix. The American legal system. New York, Harpers, 1955.

Mayers, Lewis. The American legal system. New York, Harpers, 1955.

Robertson, Reynolds and Kirkman, Francis R. Jurisdiction of the Supreme Court of the United States. Albany, Bender, 1951.

Chapter 5

HOW THE COURTS OPERATE

The papers are full of news stores of trials, both civil and criminal, but they do not furnish the readers with a picture of how the courts operate. Some knowledge of court procedures and the reasons for them is essential if we are not to be misled by the sketchy accounts of trials as they are reported by the papers. Since the jury trials which are thus reported are held in the courts of general jurisdiction, it is useful to follow a suit from beginning to end in its progress through such a court.

First Steps in a Civil Suit

In all personal actions, the court must have jurisdiction over the defendant before the case can proceed. In order to accomplish this, the plaintiff requests a summons from the clerk of the court, and has the sheriff (or other authorized person) serve it, by handing it to the defendant personally, or by leaving it with an adult at his residence or place of business. Usually the plaintiff has his statement of claim or complaint served at the same time; this procedure is subject to local court rules. The defendant has a specified time in which to answer the plaintiff's complaint. If he does not, the plaintiff has the right to have judgment entered in default. However, a defendant does not ordinarily allow this to happen. His attorney "enters an appearance", that is, files a paper indicating that he represents the defendant and that all papers may henceforth be served on him.

At this point the defendant may have several alternatives. He may believe that the statement of claim, as filed, does not state a cause of action, and he therefore files a motion to dismiss the case for that reason. If this motion is denied, he must proceed further. He may feel that the statement of claim is not definite enough, and hence ask for a bill of particulars to supply the lacking averments. Or he may be satisfied with the plaintiff's statement, and file his answer to the claim. In a personal injury suit, this is generally a denial of the allegations of the complaint, and puts at issue the relevant facts of the case. If there are no further pleadings filed, the case is put on the trial list and is reached in its regular turn.

Importance of the Jury

One characteristic common to all of the general trial courts is the jury. A jury trial has seemed so important to the states that all but a few have protected the right to a jury trial in their constitutions. From time to time the jury has been attacked as an institution which has outlived its usefulness, which slows down the processes of justice. But it remains, because the people as a whole have faith in it. The jury is the people, merely reduced in numbers.

Experience has shown that the jury system works, and that is the real test. The late Robert von Moschzisker, Chief Justice of the Pennsylvania Supreme Court, wrote of the jury: "Considering the fact that it must of necessity be administered by human beings, and therefore subject to the frailties which we all share in common, it is, to my mind, about the most perfect instrument which can be devised as an aid to organized society in administering justice between the State and its citizens and between man and man".

And the eminent New York lawyer, Joseph H. Choate, speaking from long experience as a trial lawyer, said of the jury: "For the determination of the vast majority of questions of fact, arising upon conflict of evidence, the united judgment of twelve honest and intelligent laymen, properly instructed by a wise and impartial judge, . . . is far safer and more likely to be right than the sole judgment of the same judge would be." Twelve men, from all walks of life, bring to the deliberations of the jury more experience and insight, more understanding of the motives and outlook of mankind, than can any judge, no matter how learned he may be. And the secrecy of the deliberations of the jury assures the juror freedom to vote for the plaintiff or the defendant, as he chooses, without fear of retaliation.

Choosing the Jurors

The machinery for obtaining jurors is provided for by statute. In general some public officer, such as the sheriff, or persons specifically named as jury commissioners, are authorized to prepare lists of jurors for each term of court. The names of the jurors are selected from voting lists, tax rolls or other sources. Those selected are notified by mail that they are expected to appear at a specified hour in a particular room in the court house, on the first day of their service, which is usually two weeks. At this time anyone who wishes to be excused from serving may request the presiding judge for release from duty. The courts quite properly regard duty on the jury as an obligation of citizenship, and do not often grant such requests. The jurors remaining after such applications have been heard are divided by lot into small panels or groups of thirty-six or so. When a case is ready for trial, one of these panels of jurors is escorted to the courtroom where counsel for both parties are waiting.

Selection of the Trial Jury

A court officer has the names of all the jurors on slips of paper and he selects twelve at random. As he reads off their names, the jurors take their places in the jury box in the order in which they are called. At this point the selection of the jury begins.

It might seem unnecessary to allow counsel to cull those jurors who have been so fortuitously called to serve and then further chosen by lot to form a smaller group. Why should the parties not have to take the first twelve persons whose names are called? The answer is simply that the parties are entitled to a fair and impartial trial, and this cannot be assured if counsel have no choice in the matter of which twelve of the thirty-six shall serve on the jury.

Clearly relationship or friendship with either the parties or counsel, or a prejudice might prevent an impartial trial, and counsel for the parties are entitled to obtain this information by examination of the jurors first chosen. If there appears to be some reason for the belief that a juror could not render an impartial verdict, counsel asks the judge to excuse the juror. If the court decides that this "challenge" is justified, the juror is excused and another is selected at random to take his place. In addition, each side usually has a limited number of challenges for which counsel does not have to give a reason. Thus the jury which is finally sworn in is one which both sides believe will be impartial and unbiased.

The Trial Proper

When the jury has been selected, the trial begins. The attorney for the plaintiff addresses the jury, stating what facts he expects to prove in support of plaintiff's claim. He then calls his witnesses, in the order which seems best calculated to convince the jury of the justice of his claim. After each witness is sworn, he is examined by the attorney for the plaintiff, who seeks to elicit from the witness the facts which will prove his case. When this direct examination is completed, the attorney for the defendant has an opportunity to cross-examine the witness. Cross-examination frequently enables the defense attorney to bring out facts which had not been fully disclosed before, and to point out inconsistencies in the testimony of the witness. When the plaintiff has completed the presentation of his case, the defense attorney addresses the jury in his turn, stating what he expects to prove. Then he calls his witnesses. They, too, are subject to cross-examination by the opposing counsel. Upon the completion of the presentation of the evidence by both sides, the attorneys then address the jury, summing up the evidence as they see it, and requesting the jury to find in favor of their client.

At this point the judge gives his charge to the jury. He reviews the testimony of the various witnesses, and instructs the jury with respect to the law. In some states and the Federal courts the judge may comment on the testimony of the witnesses. However, in all courts, the jury is the finder of facts, and it is their recollection of the testimony which is to guide them. At the time of the charge the attorneys may request special instructions to be added to the judge's charge. These the judge may accept or reject, subject to objections on the part of the attorney dissatisfied with the ruling. The jury then retires to the jury room for its deliberations. When it has reached its verdict, it notifies the court, and is brought back to the courtroom to announce the verdict.

Post-Trial Procedure

After the verdict is returned, the losing party may make a motion for judgment *non obstante veredicto*. This is a request that the court enter a verdict in his favor, notwithstanding the verdict brought in by the jury. It is addressed to the discretion of the court, who is asked to reverse the findings of the jury, on the grounds that the jury was palpably in error in deciding as it did. Or the losing party may ask for a new trial, on the ground that there were errors committed by the trial court which did not give the losing party the fair trial to which it was entitled. If either of these motions is granted, the opposing party may take an appeal. If they are denied, the moving party may do so.

Occasionally the party in whose favor the verdict is returned moves for a new trial, despite his victory. He may feel that the amount of the verdict is too small, and wishes to have another trial for the purpose of gaining a larger verdict. He may also feel that the rulings of the court during the trial worked to his disadvantage, and that a new trial would be advantageous to him. If his motions are denied, he may appeal; if they are granted, the opposing side may do so. At times both sides are dissatisfied with the final results of their motions, and both may appeal to the proper appellate court.

Jury Trials in Criminal Cases

The pleadings in a criminal case are simple. They consist of the indictment (the prosecution's statement of claim) and the plea of the defendant. His plea of "not guilty" is a denial of the truth of the indictment, and the jury must be satisfied as to his guilt beyond a reasonable doubt. The defendant may plead "guilty", of course, when it is apparent that a jury would convict him, and he seeks to reduce the severity of his sentence by this action.

In the selection of a jury, more time is frequently spent by both the prosecuting attorney and defense counsel. It is sometimes difficult to obtain an impartial jury in cases which have had a great deal of newspaper publicity. Time spent in such cases is not wasted, for the jurors must represent a fair sample of the citizens of the community and meet the requirements of non-bias. Few will fail to remember the trial of the communist leaders in New York City in 1949, and the months which were spent in the selection of the jury. However much this portion of the trial may have bewildered, even angered, the ordinary citizens of this country, the result was the achievement, as nearly as possible, of an impartial jury made up of men and women of all creeds, races and beliefs. Since this is requisite for a jury, the time spent was warranted by the difficulty in reaching that desideratum.

Following the verdict, the defendant may ask for a new trial: if this is refused, he may then take an appeal. If the defendant is found "not guilty", ordinarily the prosecution may not seek a new trial, for to do so would result in placing the defendant twice in jeopardy of life or limb. If the prosecution is permitted a new trial, it can only be for the reason that improper rulings of the trial court denied it the opportunity of presenting its evidence.

Trial Court Procedure

In these trial courts, the rules governing the conduct of a case seem at first glance to be artificial or unnecessary. For example, why is it necessary for the plaintiff to file a written complaint or statement of claim? Why could that not be stated in court at the time of trial? A little reflection will convince one that such a statement is necessary, so that the defendant may know in advance what is the exact nature of the plaintiff's claim. Likewise the plaintiff should be informed in advance as to the defendant's defense. Other rules of pleading have similarly logical reasons for their existence.

Rules of Evidence

Perhaps the rules with respect to the admission or rejection of evidence, and rulings by the court on the propriety of questions asked by counsel, are the most difficult for the layman to understand. Many of the rules seem aimed at keeping out information. Their purpose is, of course, quite the contrary; it is to arrive at the true facts, in an orderly and logical fashion. The difficulty lies in the conception which the layman has of what actually constitutes a fact. The rules of evidence are based on reason, and it is this which makes them seem artificial. For strangely enough, man, a reasonable being, frequently plans his conduct and arrives at conclusions on something less than reason. If Jones tells Smith that he has just seen a red truck hit a blue car in front of the grocery store, Smith's ordinary reaction would be to believe that such an event has taken place—this is a fact for Smith. But in a trial, in which this fact is a point which must be proved, Smith's testimony of the conversation, offered to prove the fact of the collision, would be excluded as hearsay.

Hearsay Evidence

Hearsay evidence can be loosely defined as "testimony in court, of a statement made out of court, by a person not present in court, such statement being offered as an assertion to show the truth of matters asserted therein, and thus resting on the credibility of the out-of-court asserter." Smith's testimony is clearly hearsay, since his testimony is being offered to prove the fact of a collision, and all he knows is what Jones told him. The truthfulness of Jones's statement does not rest on Smith, but on Jones, who is not in court. Viewed in this light, the exclusion of Smith's testimony is justified on the basis of reason. However, if the point to be proved was what Jones said, Smith's testimony is not hearsay, since Smith is testifying as to what he heard, which is the fact involved.

Thus there are several reasons for the exclusion of hearsay. One is that the person who made the hearsay statement (in our illustration, Jones) did so without the solemn obligation of an oath. A second is that the court and jury are unable to judge the demeanor of the asserter, as would be the case were he on the witness stand. Another important reason is the lack of opportunity to question this individual. The provision in constitutions that the accused shall enjoy the right to be confronted with the witnesses against him is in effect an embodiment of the hearsay rule. Although there are exceptions to this exclusory rule, these too are based on reason and experience.

Other Excluded Evidence

There are many other rules, all of which are understandable when examined in the light of reason. Testimony is excluded because it is immaterial or irrelevant. The ordinary person, in recounting events, usually introduces facts and statements which have no bearing on the events themselves, which do not contribute to an understanding of the situation being described. Such extraneous material is not received by the courts, for the reason that such material may confuse the jury and certainly wastes time, and in no way contributes to the determination of the questions involved. Similarly the courts insist on the production of documents—the "best evidence" rule—rather than relying on the recollection of a witness as to their contents.

Circumstantial Evidence

Again, evidence which is circumstantial is admitted, even though it does not immediately connect a person with an act. When crimes are committed, there is frequently no eye-witness. If circumstantial evidence were not permitted to be introduced, the guilty person would often escape conviction. Not many years ago an accused kidnapper was convicted almost entirely on circumstantial evidence. One bit of evidence which caused considerable comment was the introduction of a piece of lumber which had been found in the defendant's garage. By itself the piece of wood appeared to have no connection with the case. But an expert on lumber and timber growth testified that the piece of wood had come from the same piece of lumber which had been used to make a rail of a ladder found near the scene of the kidnapping. This innocuous bit of wood thus became one link in a chain of circumstantial evidence which resulted in the conviction of the accused.

The rules of evidence and procedure are the result of long years of experience on the part of judges. These rules have stood the test of time and the examination of critical and logical minds. Changes in them occur as experience, knowledge and science develop. Courts are always somewhat "behind the times", if popular acceptance and belief are the measure of the times. This conservatism of the courts is frequently criticized, but it is not without merit, when we consider the number of popularly accepted ideas which have proved to be without real substance. The courts may lag, but they proceed on strong and reliable grounds.

SELECTED READINGS

For further material, see Bibliography, page 121.

Callender, Clarence N. American courts; their organization and procedure. New York, McGraw-Hill, 1927.

Maguire, John MacArthur. Evidence: common sense and common law. Chicago, Foundation press, 1947.

Mayers, Lewis. The American legal system. New York, Harpers, 1955.

von Moschzisker, Robert. Trial by jury: a brief review of its origin, development and merits, and discussion of actual conduct of jury trials. Philadelphia, Bisel, 1930.

Chapter 6

MANNING THE LEGAL SYSTEM

The role of the courts in the legal system of the United States cannot be overemphasized, but it would be erroneous to think of them as constituting the system in its entirety. Courts bear much the same relationship to the legal system as hospitals do to medical service. They are available when needed, and perform a specific function. But relatively little time of lawyers, taken as a whole, is spent in court. Even those who are trying cases day after day, do more than appear in the court room. Hours must be spent in preparing for trial, in interviewing witnesses and in planning the most effective way of presenting the case in court.

In the main, lawyers spend their time in consultation with clients, in drafting documents, in advising on courses of procedure, and in investigating the state of the law on particular points. A large part of their time is spent in trying to prevent litigation, in making sure that their clients do nothing which may eventually cause disagreement, misunderstanding or difficulty. The increasing complexity of modern life has increased the need for such preventive advice. The lawyer's function is to guide us through the intricate relationships of today's living. With 48 state legislatures and court systems making law, as well as Congress and the Federal courts contributing their share, it is a task which calls for thorough and intensive training.

Law Schools and Legal Training

Preparation for the law is long, arduous and expensive. In the early days of this country, those who intended to become lawyers served an apprenticeship in the office of a member of the Bar for a period of from three to five years. In addition to assisting in office routine, these embryonic lawyers "read law", as contained in the few law books then in existence. The first law school which has had continuous existence was not founded until 1817. Slowly the number of law schools increased until today there are about 150 in the United States, with a combined enrollment of 40,000.

As this country has developed and as ease and means of communication and transportation have progressed, life has grown more complex. The importance of the training afforded by the law schools has correspondingly increased. Less than one per cent of those admitted to the Bar today have pursued their law studies in the office of a practitioner, as was done 150 years ago. As the law has continued to grow and as new areas of activity have opened up, the law schools have been obliged to increase their standard for admission. A little over 100 years ago the only entrance requirement was good character. Today most American law schools require three years of college work and many require four. The course of study has been lengthened from one year to three, and many students do post-graduate work before entering practice.

But law schools have a function beyond the mere *teaching* of law. They must prepare their students to *practice* law, to represent clients in court and at the conference table. In order to do this, law schools have had to adopt new methods of instruction and introduce new fields of study. They give courses in moot court, which may be either a simulation of a case on appeal or in the nature of a trial, complete with witnesses, judge and jury. In order that the students may get some idea of the actual day to day practice of the law, they are frequently assigned to assist in the Legal Aid Clinic, where they interview clients, write letters, prepare documents and assist practicing attorneys in the trial of cases. In some instances the law students actually conduct hearings in the lower courts. Some of the prosecuting attorneys, particularly those attached to the office of the Attorney General of the United States, use students during the summer time in their offices, giving them training in the preparation of cases, investigating matters which concern the office, and interviewing witnesses. The law schools are constantly adjusting their courses of instruction to enable their students to meet the requirements of modern practice.

However, the law schools do not limit themselves to the preparation of men and women for the practice of the law. Rightfully they have become centers for legal research. Their facilities are used in the investigation of every phase of the law, and the results of this research have been significant contributions to the effective administration of justice in this country. Law schools in large urban areas conduct courses designed especially for the practicing attorney. Some provide research and brief writing service for lawyers too far from adequate law libraries to do the work themselves. In addition, the major law schools foster law reviews, which publish articles concerning important phases and developments of the law. The law is not static, but is in a constant state of change, and these changes and their importance are almost always first pointed out in articles which appear in the law school reviews.

Admission to the Bar

Before anyone can practice law in a state, he must be admitted to the Bar of that state. Each state has its own requirements. There was no uniform system of admission in the Colonies, nor is there one now. The colonial courts controlled admission to their Bars, and usually recommendation by a member respecting the character and qualification of a prospective attorney was sufficient. Today as then control over admission lies ultimately in the courts, which are jealous of this prerogative. In all states, the highest court promulgates rules for admission to the Bar, although the administration may be delegated to other bodies. Good moral character is a prerequisite to admission to any Bar and this requirement is strictly enforced. Most states also require that the prospective attorney prove his educational qualifications by passing an examination, set by the state's Board of Bar Examiners. In view of the complexities of modern life, the educational requirements for admission to the Bar must remain high, if we are to have a Bar which is competent to handle the affairs of the American people.

Selection and Qualification of Judges

The most important single segment of any legal system is the judiciary, for upon it falls the responsibility of seeing that the system functions. High standards of character and ability are essential to the proper functioning of the courts. Although the methods of selecting the judiciary vary throughout the country, the importance of the result to the citizen is the same.

The method of selecting the Federal judiciary is prescribed in Article II, Section 2 of the Constitution and has remained unchanged since 1789. The President nominates and, with the advice and consent of the Senate the appointment is confirmed. It is understandable that the President names persons from his own political party, although this does not always happen. As in any appointment by an elected official, various pressures are brought to bear on the President when such a vacancy occurs. With respect to the Supreme Court, there is the added factor of geographical distribution of its membership. But no President has failed to recognize the gravity of the responsibility and the appointments to the Federal courts have been, through the years, on a high level.

The procedure is different in the state courts. In all of the original states, the judges were either appointed by the governor or elected by the legislature. Today, ten still follow these methods. When this country was founded, there had been little experience with universal suffrage, and *appointment* of judges seemed natural. As time went on, the new states were formed, and as the people gained confidence in themselves as voters, the method of selection of judges changed. Today most judges are elected by the people they serve. Candidates for the various state judicial positions are selected by the political parties in the same way as candidates for other public offices, and the election of judges is ordinarily on a partisan basis.

In recent years there has been a movement to make the election non-partisan; there is no indication of party affiliation on the ballot. This movement has its main strength west of the Mississippi, where thirteen of the seventeen states using this system are located. Another method of selection is being widely discussed, although it has been adopted in only two states. Under this method, the governor initially fills a vacancy on a court by appointment from a list of qualified lawyers, which has been submitted to him by a special non-partisan committee. After a year of service, the appointed judge runs for election on the basis of his record in office; his only opposition is his own performance.

The length of the term of office of a judge is as varied as the method of his selection. Federal judges are appointed, under the Federal Constitution, to serve "during good behavior." Lifetime appointment has the merit of removing judges from any pressure to curry favor with any party or group, and gives them opportunity to be unbiased and impartial. The tenure of judges in the state courts varies from state to state, and within the state a longer tenure for the appellate courts is provided than for the trial judges. Massachusetts and Rhode Island give life tenure to their judges, New Hampshire to the age of seventy, and New Jersey provides for life appointment, after an initial term of seven years. Vermont has the shortest elected term, two years, while Pennsylvania provides for an elected term of twenty-one years for the highest court, but with no right to re-election. Pennsylvania thus attempts to combine democratic election with completely impartial performance.

Strangely enough there were no qualifications for judges set out in any of the first constitutions of the original states, and Connecticut, Massachusetts and New Hampshire have not changed in this respect. The rest of the states, either by their constitutions or by statute, have a variety of requirements, such as minimum residence within the state, minimum legal experience, and minimum age, although twenty-three states have no requirement that judges of appellate courts be "learned in the law", and only thirty-three states have this as a qualification for judges of trial courts of general jurisdiction.

In view of the haphazard methods of selection and minimal requirements for qualification which prevail in the

United States, it might be assumed that the most important segment of our legal system is also the weakest. The processes of our elective systems certainly do not assure the election of the best qualified person. A political campaign cannot provide much of an evaluation of the merits of two candidates for the bench; there is little a judicial candidate can say except that he will perform the functions of his office. On the other hand, an appointive system is no guarantee of a better judiciary. Even if the appointing authority is free from all political pressures, there is no certainty that he will select the best person for the vacancy. An able trial lawyer does not always make a good trial judge, and a scholarly and brilliant office practitioner does not invariably make a good appellate judge. There is such a thing as judicial temperament, and proof of its existence must wait until a person has become a judge. When it does not exist, life tenure is a detriment to the legal system. In an elective system such errors can be corrected. On the other hand, life tenure for an outstanding judge provides him with security and assures the citizens of his services, despite the vagaries of politics. We have both systems in this country, and both seem to produce almost equally good results.

It should be borne in mind that, since judges are human, no method of selection will produce perfect results. We have had unfortunate experiences, to be sure. But the performance of our judiciary during the past 165 years has been of exceptionally high quality. There is something about the judicial robe which brings out the best in a man. Obviously it cannot change his mental ability, nor make a brilliant analyst out of a plodding thinker. But it can, and does, effect a change in his outlook and philosophy. No one can escape the sense of responsibility which comes with the oath of office. The judge's position is important to the welfare of his community, his state and the nation. No judge can escape the influence of the long line of jurists who have made the Anglo-American legal system a great tradition.

Role of the Organized Bar

The organized Bar performs an important role in all

phases of the legal profession. The American Bar Association has devoted a great deal of its attention to legal education. It has always been active in raising standards, and at present many states require that a candidate for admission be a graduate of a law school approved by the American Bar Association. The various states and local bar associations, as well, have played their roles in the movement to improve the training and proficiency of the law student.

Although control of admission to the Bar is the prerogative of the courts, the Bar of a state or locality is frequently delegated the administration of the rules regarding admission. Committees of lawyers, set up either directly by the courts or through organized bar associations, govern the procedures and examine into the fitness and character of applicants for admission. Lawyers compose the state boards of bar examiners, who determine the educational qualifications of applicants. While the courts make the ultimate determinations, they must rely, of necessity, upon these subsidiary bodies to carry out the admissions policies which the courts have set.

Discipline of members of the Bar is solely the province of the courts, but here again the Bar takes an active part in the proceedings. The American Bar Association has promulgated canons of professional ethics and these have been adopted by most courts as the rules of conduct for the members of their Bars. Supervision of the conduct of attorneys is either specifically delegated by the courts to the state or local bar associations, or is assumed by the associations through committees set up for the purpose. Where there is specific delegation, the bar association committee holds hearings upon complaints, and makes recommendations to the court respecting disciplinary action. In those instances in which the bar association acts upon its own initiative, it proceeds by means of an action before the court. In either case, the control over the discipline rests with the court; the Bar can only aid the court in its task.

Disciplinary proceedings against members of the judiciary are usually by impeachment by the state legislature, and hence the part taken by the Bar on these rare occasions is very limited. Like its canons of professional ethics, the American Bar Association has also drawn up canons of judicial ethics. These are simply standards to which the Association believes jud es should adhere. Lack of adherence does not in itself nstitute grounds for impeachment. However, these canon: lo constitute a useful measuring rod and represent one maj r aspect of the important role played by the Bar in the selection of judges. Whether judges are appointed or elected to the bench, the organized Bar of the jurisdiction attempts to prevail upon the appointing authority, the political parties and the voters to select and elect only those qualified for these responsible positions. While the associations are not always successful, their influence is significant and beneficial.

Few appointing authorities or political parties will favor for the bench any person deemed unqualified by his colleagues in the local or state bar associations, no matter how faithful to the political party the person may have been. This influence of the Bar has been particularly beneficial in maintaining the calibre of the lower state courts. It is in these lower judicial positions that political patronage is most likely to assert itself, yet it is in the lower courts that most of the controversies are settled. The importance of qualified judges in these courts is unquestionable, and the Bar has done much to promote a competent judiciary.

SELECTED READINGS

For further material, see Bibliography, page 121.

Brand, George Edward. Bar associations, attorneys and judges: organization, ethics and discipline. Chicago, American Judicature Society, 1956.

Brown, Esther Lucile. Lawyers and the promotion of justice. New York, Russell Sage Foundation, 1938.

Drinker, Henry Sandwith. Legal ethics, New York, Columbia university press, 1953.

Harno, Albert James. Legal education in the United States: a report prepared for the Survey of the Legal Profession. San Francisco, Bancroft-Whitney, 1953.

Haynes, Evan. The selection and tenure of judges. Newark, N. J., The national conference of judicial councils, 1944.

Warren, Charles. A history of the American bar. Boston, Little Brown, 1911.

Chapter 7

JUSTICE FOR ALL

This country has an excellent system of courts, administered by lawyers and judges well trained in their profession. Its hallmark is its guarantee of the personal rights of the individual. But the question remains: are these advantages enjoyed by all? Undoubtedly the person of means enjoys them. But equal justice for all means that the least fortunate as well have their rights protected fully.

Like the doctor, the lawyer does a great deal of work for which he receives no fee. However, free legal service cannot be effective when rendered on a casual basis. It requires organization. Hospitals have always existed to provide medical attention to persons with low incomes. Those requiring free legal service have had no similar organizations to aid them until recently. In a largely rural society, with its slower pace and simpler living, there was less need for legal assistance than there is in today's complex urban environment. With the increase in need, there has developed a service for those who need legal advice but who cannot afford to pay for it. This service is generally called "legal aid."

Legal Aid

The idea of legal aid does not go very far back in our history. It was first developed in New York City in the 1870's by Edward Saloman as a means of assisting his fellow-German immigrants. It has been growing ever since, until today there are over 80 legal aid services in this country. The basic concept of legal aid is an office, staffed by a permanent group of competent lawyers, who take care of the legal problems of persons who cannot afford to pay. The office may be supported as a part of some organized charity, by a department of the city, or by private funds.

The problems involved are generally not complex, but they loom large in the lives of those affected. What is needed in over eighty per cent of the cases is simply advice: only a small proportion ever get to the stage of litigation. Problems involving leases, rent, loan sharks, wills, family quarrels, installment contracts, are brought to the office, and are solved quickly and without charge. These offices supply a much needed and valuable community service and their effectiveness is only limited by the amount of support they receive.

Legal Aid Clinics

Closely allied are the legal aid clinics which are conducted by law schools in large urban areas. In these clinics the law students assist in the performance of the tasks of legal aid, under the supervision of a member of the Bar. Although the students serve without compensation, their enthusiasm for an opportunity to put their theoretical knowledge to practical use results in exceptionally competent and resourceful results.

Lawyers Referral Plan

The lawyers referral plan is a recent development to provide legal assistance to persons of moderate means, who might otherwise fail to receive the benefit of necessary legal counsel. The members of the Bar of a number of communities, realizing that there are many persons of modest income who need assistance but who cannot afford to pay the usual fee of a lawyer, have developed this type of service. Under the plan, the person in need of legal advice goes to the lawyers referral office. An appointment is made for him with one of a panel of reputable lawyers, who have agreed to consult with such clients for a modest agreed fee of perhaps $3.00. Any additional consultations and work which are necessary are at the same modest rate. The local Bar, which sponsors this service, realizes that the fees must be kept at a low level and (even more important) that the character of the service must be of the highest type. Wherever this plan has been initiated, it has proved its value to the community. Many people hesitate to consult an attorney because of the fear of the cost. When they are assured of the initial outlay, they are eager to obtain advice. And the experience has been in most instances, that advice which can be given quickly and at a saving in worry and distress, is the only thing needed.

Neighborhood Law Office

Still another kind of low cost legal service is gaining widespread acceptance—this is the neighborhood law office. Most lawyers have their offices in the center of the city, near the courts. This fact forms a barrier to the person who is employed elsewhere and who cannot afford to take time off from his job to go into the city to consult an attorney. Moreover, selecting an attorney from among the many in the downtown area is so forbidding a task that it is frequently put off. It is much easier to consult someone who has an office in one's immediate neighborhood, who is a part of that community and who is available at the hours when a client is himself free. Legal problems can be discussed and solved after five, as well as during the day. Neighborhood law offices are successful because they bring the lawyer's office into the community of the client.

Public Defender

Most of the effort of the legal aid offices has been directed to the solution of the civil affairs of their clients. In the main, these offices have not dealt with the needs of persons involved in criminal cases, largely because of lack of staff and funds. The need has always existed, and is being solved in a fashion similar to legal aid. Here again an organized program is necessary. In some communities a privately supported office to supply counsel in criminal cases has been set up. These defender organizations have gained the respect of the community by reason of their performance. Most of these privately financed groups participate in the Community Chest, an indication of the value placed on their work by the community.

The other kind is a tax-supported office, usually called the

Public Defender. Some might object to the spending of public money to defend one guilty of a crime, but it must be pointed out again that under our system there is a presumption of innocence until final conviction. The innocent are certainly entitled to defense, and if they cannot afford to employ counsel, society should provide it. The machinery for defense ought to be as adequate as that for prosecution. An organized office is the most efficient and least costly way to accomplish this desirable end. In no place where the office of Public Defender has operated for any length of time has it been discontinued, evidence that the office serves a useful and necessary purpose.

Court-Assigned Lawyers and the Bar

Development of organized legal assistance for the indigent has been relatively recent in this country, but the Sixth Amendment to the Federal Constitution has provided, since 1791, that any accused person shall enjoy the right "to have the assistance of counsel for his defense." The states have recognized this right by providing that the trial court assign counsel to the defendant in criminal cases. In most of the states this requirement applies to all classes of cases; in the remainder it applies to the more serious felonies. In some, counsel must be assigned by the court, when the defendant has no counsel to represent him. In others, counsel is assigned upon the request of the defendant. In no case, of course, is the defendant denied the right to counsel whom he retains himself. It is to the credit of the Bar that they serve when requested to do so.

It is particularly to their credit that they do not refuse to accept assignment to unpopular causes. In 1942, when the feeling against Germany was at a high pitch, a naturalized citizen of New York City was indicted for treason. The Federal District Court requested Harold R. Medina, one of the leaders of the New York City Bar, to conduct the defense of the case. Mr. Medina accepted the responsibility and, in carrying out his obligation to the court and his client, not only expended his time and money, but also suffered personal affronts and indignities. The defendant was convicted in the trial court, but on appeal to the Supreme Court of the United States, he was freed. It is noteworthy that the same government which had been defeated in this important case later appointed Mr. Medina to the Federal District Court and subsequently to the Court of Appeals.

Not only do the individual members of the Bar accept the responsibility of representing those unable to obtain counsel, but the organized bar associations recognize their obligations to supply counsel in unpopular cases, as witness the recent case in Philadelphia involving alleged Communists. The defendants made the claim that they could not find any attorney willing to defend them. The issue was so important that the Bar Association of the city, a very conservative group, decided that steps had to be taken to provide the defendants with competent counsel. As a result of its efforts, a panel of lawyers, headed by the present Chancellor of the Bar and one of the outstanding trial lawyers of the city, now represents the accused, whose rights will be as well protected as those of a man of unlimited means.

While we have not attained perfection in providing adequate legal assistance for all, it is certainly true that under the Federal and state constitutions the right to counsel is assured because the members of the Bar have demonstrated their willingness to do their share. The ultimate responsibility for the full enjoyment of this right rests in the hands of the citizens, who alone can make possible unquestioned equality for all.

SELECTED READINGS

For further material, see Bibliography, page 121.

Beaney, William Merritt. The right to counsel in American courts. Ann Arbor, University of Michigan press, 1955.

Brownell, Emery A. Legal aid in the United States. Rochester, Lawyers Co-operative, 1951.

Goldman, Mayer C. The public defender: a necessary factor in the administration of justice. New York, Putnam, 1919.

Porter, Charles Orlando. Lawyer reference plans. Boston, Survey of the legal profession, 1949.

Smith, Reginald Heber. Legal service offices for persons of moderate means. Boston, Survey of the legal profession, 1950.

EQUAL JUSTICE UNDER LAW

EPILOGUE

All over the Western World thoughtful men and women of the law are giving fresh attention these days to the meaning of the "Rule of Law." This is a wholesome thing, not only because the Rule of Law, as we know it, is being vigorously challenged in large areas of the world, but aso because its vitality in our system depends, to a considerable extent, upon broad public understanding of it.

In a simple manner of speaking, the Rule of Law means in America a government of laws instead of men. This, however, must be put down as an oversimplification. What we have and necessarily will have, even with the Rule of Law given maximum vitality, is a government of both laws and men, since men make and declare the law and men execute and enforce it. Clearly this is but recognition of reality; it is to proceed with a consciousness of human limitations.

I shall leave it to others to attempt more explicit restatement, but I do want to mention certain elements, which are, in my judgment, of great moment in the unending struggle to approach in conception and application the ideal of the Rule of Law. The first of these is separation of powers and checks and balances in government. They tend to bring about the second element, a reasonable degree of objectivity in the formulation of the substantive law, that is, the body of law which governs the relations of man to man and man to government. The law-making body in enacting statutory law is concerned with giving it understandable content both for the citizen and for the governmental agencies concerned with its application and enforcement.

The third element is substantive limitations on governmental authority in relation to individuals. These embrace constitutional protections for the individual with respect to his mind, spirit (religion), person and property. They are closely related to the fourth, namely, basic requirements of fair procedure, designed to assure fairness in the application of law to the individual. Finally there are the elements of an independent judiciary and an independent Bar.

The problem of giving a genuine measure of objectivity to the substantive law has been greatly aggravated by the conditions of contemporary society. The basic ideas which underlie much of our private law and our criminal law have been validated by many generations of experience. They, thus, have a solid element of principle which is helpful, in terms both of popular understanding and conformance and of guidance of those charged with their application. The growing body of regulatory law, which has been occasioned by the complexity and interdependence of human affairs, presents a greater problem since it is shaped to meet problems as they arise in a fast-changing society and cannot fairly be said to be grounded on a solid footing of principle or experience. Since completely detailed specification is generally neither practicable nor desirable in regulatory measures, the tendency in the growth of our law has been to provide a considerable measure of administrative discretion in the very spelling out of the rules of the game and to safeguard the individual, both by affording opportunity to be heard in connection with the adoption of substantive rules and effective procedural safeguards in relation to the application of the rules. In the last analysis, the practical strength of procedural safeguards is likely to depend on the availability of judicial review of administrative action.

Over a long period we in America have succeeded in developing rules of fair procedure for judicial proceedings which do our legal system much credit. The Bill of Rights early expressed basic rules of fair play, notably in the Fifth and Sixth Amendments. Much more recently we have been making progress along these lines in connection with the administrative process. Even more recently this subject has been brought sharply into public focus in connection with the investigatory phase of the legislative process. It is good to note that progress is being made here, although thinking and governmental action on this part of the work of the legislative bodies has not been brought to full maturity.

In a discussion of the Rule of Law fair procedure deserves particular attention, both because the finest constitutional pronouncements about human rights may be empty rhetoric in the absence of procedural safeguards and because, in the heat of public controversy, it is easy to get impatient with the employment of procedural guaranties in behalf of people who appear unworthy or odious. As for the first question, one can say with considerable confidence that procedural safeguards are vital to human liberty; they are perhaps more than anything else characteristic of the genius of Anglo-American law.

One can readily illustrate the second point be reference to the privilege against self-incrimination, which is one of a number of constitutional safeguards provided by the Fifth Amendment. In our system of criminal justice an individual is presumed to be innocent of crime until the state, in an orderly judicial proceeding, establishes beyond a reasonable doubt that he is guilty. The privilege against self-incrimination is a necessary concomitant; without it the individual could be forced to help the state make out a case against all; the question of guilt is a matter of proof and, regardless of the ultimate fact of guilt or innocence, the individual cannot be compelled to give testimony tending to make out even by circumstantial evidence that he had committed a crime. This being so, the Rule of Law would break down were were to fail to respect the privilege, however odious an individual who invokes the privilege may be in the eyes of many of us.

As Justice Brandeis put it, "the supremacy of the law demands that there shall be opportunity to have some court decide whether an erroneous rule of law was applied; and whether the proceedings in which facts were adjudicated was conducted regularly." He undoubtedly meant "some *independent* court" since the significance of the judicial function he was stressing depends upon the integrity of the courts and their processes. The point Brandeis made carries beyond the statute law; it goes to the fundamental law, including the Bill of Rights as well. At that level the handmaiden of an independent judiciary is the power of the courts to determine whether legislative and executive action consists with the Constitution. Without this power the Supreme Court of the United States could not have enforced constitutional safeguards for the individual and would not stand today as the great protector of civil liberty.

The existence of an independent Bar is as indispensable to

the preservation of the Rule of Law as is the presence of an independent judiciary. Without counsel free to represent an individual to the best of his ability, substantive and procedural safeguards would exist in theory but not in practice. The right to counsel, moreover, is universal; to deny it to anyone is to compromise the Rule of Law. One may well add that to apply economic sanctions to a lawyer who has the courage to represent unpopular persons and causes is to attack the independence of the Bar and, thus, to attack indirectly the Rule of Law.

The outlook for an even closer approach to the ideal of equal justice under law in the United States is favorable. Despite cross currents, there has been substantial progress toward underlying social and economic justice. There exists in the politico-legal system all the elements, important to the realization of the Rule of Law, which have been considered. A tremendously invigorating force has been the sensitive and courageous interpretation and application of the Bill of Rights and related provisions by the Supreme Court of the United States. With increased public understanding of these things, the advancement of the common good without invasion or sacrifice of fundamental individual values is assured.

JEFFERSON B. FORDHAM

Appendix A:

CONSTITUTIONAL GUARANTIES; DOCUMENTS AND COMPARATIVE TABLE

VIRGINIA DECLARATION OF RIGHTS
(Adopted June 12, 1776)

A DECLARATION of RIGHTS made by the representatives of the good people of Virginia, assembled in full and free Convention; which rights do pertain to them, and their posterity, as the basis and foundation of government.

1. That all men are by nature equally free and independent, and have certain inherent rights, of which, when they enter into a state of society, they cannot, by any compact, deprive or divest their posterity; namely, the enjoyment of life and liberty, with the means of acquiring and possessing property, and pursuing and obtaining happiness and safety.

2. That all power is vested in, and consequently derived from, the people; that magistrates are their trustees and servants, and at all times amenable to them.

3. That government is, or ought to be, instituted for the common benefit, protection, and security, of the people, nation, or community, of all the various modes and forms of government that is best, which is capable of producing the greatest degree of happiness and safety, and is most effectually secured against the danger of maladministration; and that whenever any government shall be found inadequate or contrary to these purposes, a majority of the community hath an indubitable, unalienable, and indefeasible right, to reform, alter, or abolish it, in such manner as shall be judged most conducive to the publick weal.

4. That no man, or set of men, are entitled to exclusive or separate emoluments or privileges from the community, but in consideration of publick services; which, not being descendible, neither ought the offices of magistrate, legislator, or judge, to be hereditary.

5. That the legislative and executive powers of the state should be separate and distinct from the judiciary; and, that the members of the two first may be restrained from oppression, by feeling and participating the burthens of the people, they should, at fixed periods, be reduced to a private station, return into that body from which they were originally taken, and the vacancies be supplied by frequent, certain, and regular elections, in which all, or any part of the former members, to be again eligible, or ineligible, as the laws shall direct.

6. That elections of members to serve as representatives of the people, in assembly, ought to be free; and that all men, having sufficient evidence of permanent common interest with, and attachment to, the community, have the right of suffrage, and cannot be taxed or deprived of their property for publick uses without their own consent, or that of their representatives so elected, nor bound by any law to which they have not, in like manner, assented for the publick good.

7. That all power of suspending laws, or the execution of laws, by any authority without consent of the representatives of the people, is injurious to their rights, and ought not to be exercised.

8. That in all capital or criminal prosecution a man hath a right to demand the cause and nature of his accusation, to be confronted with the accusers and witnesses, to call for evidence in his favour, and to a speedy trial by an impartial jury of his vicinage, without whose unanimous consent he cannot be found guilty, nor can he be compelled to give evidence against himself; that no man be deprived of his liberty except by the law of the land, or the judgment of his peers.

9. That excessive bail ought not to be required, no excessive fines imposed, nor cruel and unusual punishments inflicted.

10. That general warrants, whereby any officer or messenger may be commanded to search suspected places without evidence of a fact committed, or to seize any person or persons not named, or whose offence is not particularly described and supported by evidence, are grievous and oppressive, and ought not to be granted.

11. That in controversies respecting property, and in suits between man and man, the ancient trial by jury is preferable to any other, and ought to be held sacred.

12. That the freedom of the press is one of the great bulwarks of liberty, and can never be restrained but by despotick governments.

13. That a well regulated militia, composed of the body of the people, trained to arms, is the proper, natural, and safe defence of a free state; that standing armies, in time of peace, should be avoided, as dangerous to liberty; and that, in all cases, the military should be under strict subordination to, and governed by, the civil power.

14. That the people have a right to uniform government; and therefore, that no government separate from, or independent of, the government of Virginia, ought to be erected or established within the limits thereof.

15. That no free government, or the blessings of liberty, can be preserved to any people but by a firm adherence to justice, moderation, temperance, frugality, and virtue, and by frequent recurrence to fundamental principles.

16. That religion, or the duty which we owe to our CREATOR, and the manner of discharging it, can be directed only by reason and conviction, not by force or violence; and therefore all men are equally entitled to the free exercise of religion, according to the dictates of conscience; and that it is the mutual duty of all to practise Christian forbearance, love, and charity, towards each other.

THE FEDERAL BILL OF RIGHTS
(Proclaimed December 15, 1791)

Article I

Congress shall make no law respecting an establishment of religion, or prohibiting the free exercise thereof; or abridging the freedom of speech, or of the press; or the right of the people peaceably to assemble, and to petition the Government for a redress of grievances.

Article II

A well-regulated Militia being necessary to the security of a free State, the right of the people to keep and bear Arms shall not be infringed.

Article III

No soldier shall, in time of peace be quartered in any house, without the consent of the Owner, nor in time of war, but in a manner to be prescribed by law.

Article IV

The right of the people to be secure in their persons, houses, papers, and effects, against unreasonable searches and seizures, shall not be violated, and no Warrants shall issue, but upon probable cause, supported by Oath or affirmation, and particularly describing the place to be searched, and the person or things to be seized.

Article V

No person shall be held to answer for a capital, or otherwise infamous crime, unless on a presentment or indictment of a Grand Jury, except in cases arising in the land or naval forces, or in the Militia, when in actual service in time of War or public danger; nor shall any person be subject for the same offense to be twice put in jeopardy of life or limb; nor shall be compelled in any criminal case to be a witness against himself, nor be deprived of life, liberty, or property, without due process of law; nor shall private property be taken for public use, without just compensation.

Article VI

In all criminal prosecutions, the accused shall enjoy the right to a speedy and public trial, by an impartial jury of the State and District wherein the crime shall have been committed, which district shall have been previously ascertained by law, and to be informed of the nature and cause of the accusation; to be confronted with the witnesses against him; to have compulsory process for obtaining witnesses in his favor, and to have the Assistance of Council for his defense.

Article VII

In Suits at common law, where the value in controversy shall exceed twenty dollars, the right of trial by jury shall be preserved, and no fact tried by a jury, shall be otherwise re-examined in any Court of the United States, than according to the rules of the common law.

Article VIII

Excessive bail shall not be required, nor excessive fines imposed, nor cruel and unusual punishments inflicted.

Article IX

The enumeration in the Constitution of certain rights shall not be construed to deny or disparage others retained by the people.

Article X

The powers not delegated to the United States by the Constitution, nor prohibited by it to the States, are reserved to the States respectively, or to the people.

PERSONAL RIGHTS AND LIBERTIES SPECIFICALLY PROVIDED FOR IN STATE AND FEDERAL BILL OF RIGHTS

The rights and liberties of the Federal Bill of Rights are listed in the order in which they appear in the first ten amendments. The privilege of the writ of habeas corpus, which is found in Article I, Section 9 of the Federal Constitution, is included because it is found in all but three of the state Bills of Rights. The right to bail is included for the same reason.

Freedom of religion: All.

Freedom of speech: All but Delaware, North Carolina and Rhode Island.

Freedom of the press: All.

Freedom to assemble: All but Maryland, Minnesota, New Mexico, Utah and Virginia.

Right to bear arms: All but California, Delaware, Illinois, Iowa, Maryland, Minnesota, Nebraska, Nevada, New Jersey, New York, North Dakota, Virginia, West Virginia, Wisconsin.

No quartering of troops: All but Florida, Louisiana, Minnesota, Mississippi, New York, Vermont, Virginia, Wisconsin.

No unreasonable search and seizure: All.

Grand jury indictment: All but Georgia, Indiana, Kansas, Massachusetts, Michigan, Minnesota, New Hampshire, Oregon, Vermont, Virginia, Wisconsin.

No double jeopardy: All but Connecticut, Marqland, Massachusetts, North Carolina, Vermont.

No self-incrimination: All but Iowa and New Jersey.

Due process: All but Indiana, Kansas, Oregon.

Taking property without compensation: All but Kansas, Michigan: provided for elsewhere in Vermont.

Speedy criminal jury trial: All but Nevada.

Knowledge of accusation: All but Nevada and North Dakota.

Confrontation of witnesses: All but Colorado, Nevada and North Dakota.

Compulsory attendance of witnesses: All but Nevada.

Right to counsel: All.

Right to civil jury trial. All but Louisiana.

No excessive bail: All but Illinois: provided for elsewhere in Vermont.

No excessive fines: All but Illinois and Vermont.

No cruel and unusual punishments: All but Connecticut, Illinois, Vermont.

Habeas corpus: All but Maryland, Massachusetts and Vermont, which provide for this right elsewhere in their constitutions.

Right to bail: All but United States, Maryland, Massachusetts, Virginia, West Virginia: provided for elsewhere in Vermont.

Appendix B:

CHARTS OF THE FEDERAL COURTS AND A STATE COURT SYSTEM

UNITED STATES COURTS

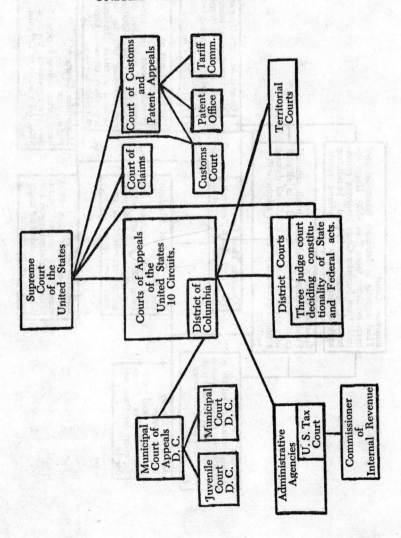

COURTS OF PENNSYLVANIA

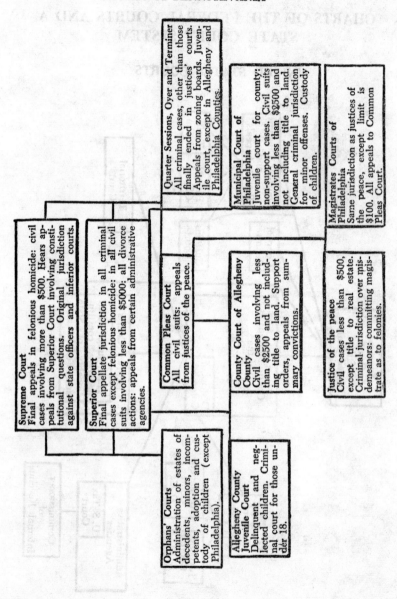

Supreme Court
Final appeals in felonious homicide; civil cases involving more than $500. Hears appeals from Superior Court involving constitutional questions. Original jurisdiction against state officers and inferior courts.

Superior Court
Final appellate jurisdiction in all criminal cases except felonious homicide; in all civil suits involving less than $5000; all divorce actions; appeals from certain administrative agencies.

Quarter Sessions, Oyer and Terminer
All criminal cases, other than those finally ended in justices' courts. Appeals from zoning boards. Juvenile court, except in Allegheny and Philadelphia Counties.

Municipal Court of Philadelphia
Juvenile court for county; non-support cases. Civil suits involving less than $2500 and not including title to land. General criminal jurisdiction for minor offenses. Custody of children.

Magistrates Courts of Philadelphia
Same jurisdiction as justices of the peace, except limit is $100. All appeals to Common Pleas Court.

Common Pleas Court
All civil suits; appeals from justices of the peace.

County Court of Allegheny County
Civil cases involving less than $2500 and not including title to land. Support orders, appeals from summary convictions.

Justice of the peace
Civil cases less than $500, except title to real estate. Criminal jurisdiction over misdemeanors; committing magistrate as to felonies.

Orphans' Courts
Administration of estates of decedents, minors, incompetents, adoption and custody of children (except Philadelphia).

Allegheny County Juvenile Court
Delinquent and neglected children. Criminal court for those under 18.

Appendix C:

AMERICAN BAR ASSOCIATION.
CANONS OF JUDICIAL AND PROFESSIONAL ETHICS

CANONS OF JUDICIAL ETHICS

PREAMBLE

In addition to the Canons for Professional Conduct of Lawyers which it has formulated and adopted, the American Bar Association, mindful that the character and conduct of a judge should never be objects of indifference, and that declared ethical standards tend to become habits of life, deems it desirable to set forth its views respecting those principles which should govern the personal practice of members of the judiciary in the administration of their office. The Association accordingly adopts the following Canons, the spirit of which it suggests as a proper guide and reminder for judges, and as indicating what the people have a right to expect from them.

1. RELATIONS OF THE JUDICIARY.

The assumption of the office of judge casts upon the incumbent duties in respect to his personal conduct which concern his relation to the state and its inhabitants, the litgants before him, the principles of law, the practitioners of law in his court, and the witnesses, jurors and attendants who aid him in the administration of its functions.

2. THE PUBLIC INTEREST.

Courts exist to promote justice, and thus to serve the public interest. Their administration should be speedy and careful. Every judge should at all times be alert in his rulings and in the conduct of the business of the court, so far as he can, to make it useful to litigants and to the community. He should avoid unconsciously falling into the attitude of mind that the litigants are made for the courts instead of the courts for the litigants.

3. Constitutional Obligations.

It is the duty of all judges in the United States to support the federal Constitution and that of the state whose laws they administer; in so doing, they should fearlessly observe and apply fundamental limitations and guarantees.

4. Avoidance of Impropriety.

A judge's official conduct should be free from impropriety and the appearance of impropriety; he should avoid infractions of law; and his personal behavior, not only upon the Bench and in the performance of judicial duties, but also in his every day life, should be beyond reproach.

5. Essential Conduct.

A judge should be temperate, attentive, patient, impartial, and, since he is to administer the law and apply it to the facts, he should be studious of the principles of the law and diligent in endeavoring to ascertain the facts.

6. Industry.

A judge should exhibit an industry and application commensurate with the duties imposed upon him.

7. Promptness.

A judge should be prompt in the performance of his judicial duties, recognizing that the time of litigants, jurors and attorneys is of value, and that habitual lack of punctuality on his part justifies dissatisfaction with the administration of the business of the court.

8. Court Organization.

A judge should organize the court with a view to the prompt and convenient dispatch of its business and he should not tolerate abuses and neglect by clerks, and other assistants who are sometimes prone to presume too much upon his good natured acquiescence by reason of friendly association with him.

It is desirable too, where the judicial system permits, that he should co-operate with other judges of the same court, and in other courts, as members of a single judicial system, to promote the more satisfactory administration of justice.

9. CONSIDERATION FOR JURORS AND OTHERS.

A judge should be considerate of jurors, witnesses and others in attendance upon the court.

10. COURTESY AND CIVILITY.

A judge should be courteous to counsel, especially in those who are young and inexperienced, and also to all others appearing or concerned in the administration of justice in the court.

He should also require, and, so far as his power extends, enforce on the part of clerks, court officers and counsel civility and courtesy to the court and to jurors, witnesses, litigants and others having business in the court.

11. UNPROFESSIONAL CONDUCT OF ATTORNEYS AND COUNSEL.

A judge should utilize his opportunities to criticise and correct unprofessional conduct of attorneys and counsellors, brought to his attention; and, if adverse comment is not a sufficient corrective, should send the matter at once to the proper investigating and disciplinary authorities.

12. APPOINTEES OF THE JUDICIARY AND THEIR COMPENSATION.

Trustees, receivers, masters, referees, guardians and other persons appointed by a judge to aid in the administration of justice should have the strictest probity and impartiality and should be selected with a view solely to their character and fitness. The power of making such appointments should not be exercised by him for personal or partisan advantage. He should not permit his appointments to be controlled by others than himself. He should also avoid nepotism and undue favoritism in his appointments.

While not hesitating to fix or approve just amounts, he should be most scrupulous in granting or approving compensation for the services or charges of such appointees to avoid excessive allowances, whether or not expected to or complained of. He cannot rid himself of this responsibility by the consent of counsel.

13. KINSHIP OR INFLUENCE.

A judge should not act in a controversy where a near relative is a party; he should not suffer his conduct to justify the impression that any person can improperly influence him or unduly enjoy his favor, or that he is affected by the kinship, rank, position or influence of any party or other person.

14. INDEPENDENCE.

A judge should not be swayed by partisan demands, public clamor or considerations of personal popularity or notoriety, nor be apprehensive of unjust criticism.

15. INTERFERENCE IN CONDUCT OF TRIAL.

A judge may properly intervene in a trial of a case to promote expedition, and prevent unnecessary waste of time, or to clear up some obscurity, but he should bear in mind that his undue interference, impatience, or participation in the examination of witnesses, or a severe attitude on his part toward witnesses, especially those who are excited or terrified by the unusual circumstances of a trial, may tend to prevent the proper presentation of the cause, or the ascertainment of the truth in respect thereto.

Conversation between the judge and counsel in court is often necessary, but the judge should be studious to avoid controversies which are apt to obscure the merits of the dispute between litigants and lead to its unjust disposition. In addressing counsel, litigants, or witnesses, he should avoid a controversial manner or tone.

He should avoid interruptions of counsel in their arguments except to clarify his mind as to their positions, and he should not be tempted to the unnecessary display of learning or a premature judgment.

16. EX PARTE APPLICATIONS.

A judge should discourage ex parte hearings of applications for injunctions and receiverships where the order may work detriment to absent parties; he should act upon such ex parte applications only where the necessity for quick action is clearly shown; if this be demonstrated, then he should endeavor to counteract the effect of the absence of opposing counsel by a scrupulous cross-examination and investigation as to the facts and the principles of law on which the application is based, granting relief only when fully satisfied that the law permits it and the emergency demands it. He should remember that an injunction is a limitation upon the freedom of action of defendants and should not be granted lightly or inadvisedly. One applying for such relief must sustain the burden of showing clearly its necessity and this burden is increased in the absence of the party whose freedom of action is sought to be restrained even though only temporarily.

17. EX PARTE COMMUNICATIONS.

A judge should not permit private interviews, arguments or communications designed to influence his judicial action, where interests to be affected thereby are not represented before him, except in cases where provision is made by law for ex parte application.

While the conditions under which briefs of argument are to be received are largely matters of local rule or practice, he should not permit the contents of such brief presented to him to be concealed from opposing counsel. Ordinarily all communications of counsel to the judge intended or calculated to influence action should be made known to opposing counsel.

18. CONTINUANCES.

Delay in the administration of justice is a common cause of complaint; counsel are frequently responsible for this delay. A judge, without being arbitrary or forcing cases unreasonably or unjustly to trial when unprepared, to the detriment of parties, may well endeavor to hold counsel to a proper appreciation of their duties to the public interest, to their own clients, and to the adverse party and his counsel, so as to enforce due diligence in the dispatch of business before the court.

19. JUDICIAL OPINIONS.

In disposing of controverted cases, a judge should indicate the reasons for his action in an opinion showing that he has not disregarded or overlooked serious arguments of counsel. He thus shows his full understanding of the case, avoids the suspicion of arbitrary conclusion, promotes confidence in his intellectual integrity and may contribute useful precedent to the growth of the law.

It is desirable that Courts of Appeal in reversing cases and granting new trials should so indicate their views on questions of law argued before them and necessarily arising in the controversy that upon the new trial counsel may be aided to avoid the repetition of erroneous positions of law and shall not be left in doubt by the failure of the court to decide such questions.

But the volume of reported decisions is such and is so rapidly increasing that in writing opinions which are to be published judges may well take this fact into consideration, and curtail them accordingly, without substantially departing from the principles stated above.

It is of high importance that judges constituting a court of last resort should use effort and self-restraint to promote solidarity of conclusion and the consequent influence of judicial decision. A judge should not yield to pride of opinion or value more highly his individual reputation than that of the court to which he should be loyal. Except in case of conscientious difference of opinion on fundamental principle, dissenting opinions should be discouraged in courts of last resort.

20. Influence of Decisions Upon the Development of the Law.

A judge should be mindful that his duty is the application of general law to particular instances, that ours is a government of law and not of men, and that he violated his duty as a minister of justice under such a system if he seeks to do what he may personally consider substantial justice in a particular case and disregards the general law as he knows it to be binding on him. Such action may become a precedent unsettling accepted principles and may have detrimental consequences beyond the immediate controversy.

He should administer his office with a due regard to the integrity of the system of the law itself, remembering that he is not a depositary of arbitrary power, but a judge under the sanction of law.

21. IDIOSYNCRASIES AND INCONSISTENCIES.

Justice should not be moulded by the individual idiosyncrasies of those who administer it. A judge should adopt the usual and expected method of doing justice, and not seek to be extreme or peculiar in his judgments, or spectacular or sensational in the conduct of the court. Though vested with discretion in the imposition of mild or severe sentences he should not compel persons brought before him to submit to some humiliating act or discipline of his own devising, without authority of law, because he thinks it will have a beneficial corrective influence.

In imposing sentence he should endeavor to conform to a reasonable standard of punishment and should not seek popularity or publicity either by exceptional severity or undue leniency.

22. REVIEW.

In order that a litigant may secure the full benefit of the right of review accorded to him by law, a trial judge should scrupulously grant to the defeated party opportunity to present the questions arising upon the trial exactly as they arose, were presented, and decided, by full and fair bill of exceptions or otherwise; any failure in this regard on the part of the judge is peculiarly worthy of condemnation because the wrong done may be irremediable.

23. LEGISLATION.

A judge has exceptional opportunity to observe the operation of statutes, especially those relating to practice, and to ascertain whether they tend to impede the just disposition of controversies; and he may well contribute to the public interest by advising those having authority to remedy defects of procedure, of the result of his observation and experience.

24. Inconsistent Obligations.

A judge should not accept inconsistent duties; not incur obligations, pecuniary or otherwise, which will in any way interfere or appear to interfere with his devotion to the expeditious and proper administration of his official funtions.

25. Business Promotions and Solicitations for Charity.

A judge should avoid giving ground for any reasonable suspicion that he is utilizing the power or prestige of his office to persuade or coerce others to patronize or contribute, either to the success of private business ventures, or to charitable enterprises. He should, therefore, not enter into such private business, or pursue such a course of conduct, as would justify such suspicion, not use the power of his office or the influence of his name to promote the business interests of others; he should not solicit for charities, nor should he enter into any business relation which, in the normal course of events reasonably to be expected, might bring his personal interest into conflict with the impartial performance of his official duties.

26. Personal Investments and Relations.

A judge should abstain from making personal investments in enterprises which are apt to be involved in litigation in the court; and, after his accession to the Bench, he should not retain such investments previously made, longer than a period sufficient to enable him to dispose of them without serious loss. It is desirable that he should, so far as reasonably possible, refrain from all relations which would normally tend to arouse the suspicion that such relations warp or bias his judgment, or prevent his impartial attitude of mind in the administration of his judicial duties.

He should not utilize information coming to him in a judicial capacity for purposes of speculation; and it detracts from the public confidence in his integrity and the soundness of his judicial judgment for him at any time to become a speculative investor upon the hazard of a margin.

27. EXECUTORSHIPS AND TRUSTEESHIPS.

While a judge is not disqualified from holding executorships or trusteeships, he should not accept or continue to hold any fiduciary or other position if the holding of it would interfere or seem to interfere with the proper performance of his judicial duties, or if the business interests of those represented require investments in enterprises that are apt to come before him judicially, or to be involved in questions of law to be determined by him.

28. PARTISAN POLITICS.

While entitled to entertain his personal views of political questions, and while not required to surrender his rights or opinions as a citizen, it is inevitable that suspicion of being warped by political bias will attach to a judge who becomes the active promoter of the interests of one political party as against another. He should avoid making political speeches, making or soliciting payment of assessments or contributions to party funds, the public endorsement of candidates for political office and participation in party conventions.

He should neither accept nor retain a place on any party committee nor act as a party leader, nor engage generally in partisan activities.

Where, however, it is necessary for judges to be nominated and elected as candidates of a political party, nothing herein contained shall prevent the judge from attending or speaking at political gatherings, or from making contributions to the campaign funds of the party that has nominated him and seeks his election or re-election.

29. SELF-INTEREST.

A judge should abstain from performing or taking part in any judicial act in which his personal interests are involved. If he has personal litigation in the court of which he is judge, he need not resign his judgeship on that account, but he should, of course, refrain from any judicial act in such a controversy.

30. CANDIDACY FOR OFFICE.

A candidate for judicial position should not make or suffer others to make for him, promises of conduct in office which appeal to the cupidity or prejudices of the appointing or electing power; he should not announce in advance his conclusions of law on disputed issues to secure class support, and he should do nothing while a candidate to create the impression that if chosen, he will administer his office with bias, partiality or improper discrimination.

While holding a judicial position he should not become an active candidate either at a party primary or at a general election for any office other than a judicial office. If a judge should decide to become a candidate for any office not judicial, he should resign in order that it cannot be said that he is using the power or prestige of his judicial position to promote his own candidacy or the success of his party.

If a judge becomes a candidate for any judicial office, he should refrain from all conduct which might tend to arouse reasonable suspicion that he is using the power or prestige of his judicial position to promote his candidacy or the success of his party.

He should not permit others to do anything in behalf of his candidacy which would reasonably lead to such suspicion.

31. PRIVATE LAW PRACTICE.

In many states the practice of law by one holding judicial position is forbidden. In superior courts of general jurisdiction, it should never be permitted. In inferior courts in some states, it is permitted because the county or municipality is not able to pay adequate living compensation for a competent judge. In such cases one who practices law is in a position of great delicacy and must be scrupulously careful to avoid conduct in his practice whereby he utilizes or seems to utilize his judicial position to further his professional success.

He should not practise in the court in which he is a judge, even when presided over by another judge, or appear therein for himself in any controversy.

If forbidden to practise law, he should refrain from accepting any professional employment while in office.

He may properly act as arbitrator or lecture upon or instruct in law, or write upon the subject, and accept compensation therefor, if such course does not interfere with the due performance of his judicial duties, and is not forbidden by some positive provision of law.

32. Gifts and Favors.

A judge should not accept any presents or favors from litigants, or from lawyers practising before him or from others whose interests are likely to be submitted to him for judgment.

33. Social Relations.

It is not necessary to the proper performance of judicial duty that a judge should live in retirement or seclusion; it is desirable that, so far as reasonable attention to the completion of his work will permit, he continue to mingle in social intercourse, and that he should not discontinue his interest in or appearance at meetings of members of the Bar. He should, however, in pending or prospective litigation before him be particularly careful to avoid such action as may reasonably tend to awaken the suspicion that his social or business relations or friendships constitute an element in influencing his judicial conduct.

34. A Summary of Judicial Obligation.

In every particular his conduct should be above reproach. He should be conscientious, studious, thorough, courteous, patient, punctual, just, impartial, fearless of public clamor, regardless of public praise, and indifferent to private political or partisan influences; he should administer justice according to law, and deal with his appointments as a public trust; he should not allow other affairs or his private interests to interfere with the prompt and proper performance of his judicial duties, nor should he administer the office for the purpose of advancing his personal ambitions or increasing his popularity.

35. Improper Publicizing of Court Procceedings.

Proceedings in court should be conducted with fitting dignity and decorum. The taking of photographs in the court room, during sessions of the court or recesses between sessions, and the broadcasting or televising of court proceedings are calculated to detract from the essential dignity of the proceedings, distract the witness in giving his testimony, degrade the court, and create misconceptions with respect thereto in the mind of the public and should not be permitted.

Provided that this restriction shall not apply to the broadcasting or televising, under the supervision of the court, of such portions of naturalization proceedings (other than the interrogation of applicants) as are designed and carried out exclusively as a ceremony for the purpose of publicity demonstrating in an impressive manner the essential dignity and the serious nature of naturalization.

36. Conduct of Court Proceedings.

Proceedings in court should be so conducted as to reflect the importance and seriousness of the inquiry to ascertain the truth.

The oath should be administered to witnesses in a manner calculated to impress them with the importance and solemnity of their promise to adhere to the truth. Each witness should be sworn separately and impressively at the bar or the court, and the clerk should be required to make a formal record of the administration of the oath, including the name of the witness.

CANONS OF PROFESSIONAL ETHICS

Preamble

In America, where the stability of Courts and of all departments of government rests upon the approval of the people, it is peculiarly essential that the system for establishing and dispensing Justice be developed to a high point of efficiency and so maintained that the public shall have absolute confidence in the integrity and impartiality of its administration. The future of the Republic, to a great extent, depends upon our maintenance of Justice pure and unsullied. It cannot be so maintained unless the conduct and the motives of all members of our profession are such as to medit the approval of all just men.

No code or set of rules can be framed, which will particularize all the duties of the lawyer in the varying phases of litigation or in all the relations of professional life. The following canons of ethics are adopted by the American Bar Association as a general guide, yet the enumeration of particular duties should not be construed as denial of the existence of others equally imperative, though not specifically mentioned.

1. The Duty of the Lawyers to the Courts

It is the duty of the lawyer to maintain towards the courts a respectful attitude, not for the sake of the temporary incumbent of the judicial office but for the maintenance of its supreme importance. Judges, not being wholly free to defend themselves, are peculiarly entitled to receive the support of the Bar against unjust criticism and clamor. Whenever there is proper ground for serious complaint of a judicial officer, it is the right and duty of the lawyer to submit his grievances to the proper authorities. In such cases, but not otherwise, such charges should be encouraged and the person making them should be protected.

2. The Selection of Judges

It is the duty of the Bar to endeavor to prevent political considerations from outweighing judicial fitness in the selection of Judges. It should protest earnestly and actively against the appointment or election of those who are unsuitable for the Bench; and it should strive to have elevated thereto only those willing to forego other employments, whether of a business, political or other character, which may embarrass their free and fair consideration of questions before them for decision. The aspiration of lawyers for judicial position should be governed by an impartial estimate of their ability to add honor to the office and not by a desire for the distinction the position may bring to themselves.

3. ATTEMPTS TO EXERT PERSONAL INFLUENCE ON THE COURT

Marked attention and unusual hospitality on the part of a lawyer to a Judge, uncalled for by the personal relations of the parties, subject both the Judge and the lawyer to misconstructions of motive and should be avoided. A lawyer should not communicate or argue privately with the Judge as to the merits of a pending cause, and he deserves rebuke and denunciation for any device or attempt to gain from a Judge special personal consideration or favor. A self-respecting independence in the discharge of professional duty, without denial or diminution of the courtesy and respect due the Judge's station, is the only proper foundation for cordial personal and official relations between Bench and Bar.

4. WHEN COUNSEL FOR AN INDIGENT PRISONER

A lawyer assigned as counsel for an indigent prisoner ought not to ask to be excused for any trivial reason, and should always exert his best efforts in his behalf.

5. THE DEFENSE OR PROSECUTION OF THOSE ACCUSED OF CRIME

It is the right of the lawyer to undertake the defense of a person accused of crime, regardless of his personal opinion as to the guilt of the accused; otherwise innocent persons, victims only of suspicious circumstances, might be denied proper defense. Having undertaken such defense, the lawyer is bound by all fair and honorable means, to present every defense that the law of the land permits, to the end that no person may be deprived of life or liberty, but by due process of law.

The primary duty of a lawyer engaged in public prosecution is not to convict, but to see that justice is done. The suppression of facts or the secreting of witnesses capable of establishing the innocence of the accused is highly reprehensible.

6. ADVERSE INFLUENCES AND CONFLICTING INTERESTS

It is the duty of a lawyer at the time of retainer to disclose to the client all the circumstances of his relations to the parties, and any interest in or connection with the controversy, which might influence the client in the selection of counsel.

It is unprofessional to represent conflicting interests, except by express consent of all concerned given after a full disclosure of the facts. Within the meaning of this canon, a lawyer represents conflicting interests when, in behalf of one client, it is his duty to contend for that which duty to another client requires him to oppose.

The obligation to represent the client with undivided fidelity and not to divulge his secrets or confidences forbids also the subsequent acceptance of retainers or employment from others in matters adversely affecting any interest of the client with respect to which confidence has been reposed.

7. PROFESSIONAL COLLEAGUES AND CONFLICTS OF OPINION

A client's proffer of assistance of additional counsel should not be regarded as evidence of want of confidence, but the matter should be left to the determination of the client. A lawyer should decline association as colleague if it is objectionable to the original counsel, but if the lawyer first retained is relieved, another may come into the case.

When lawyers jointly associated in a cause cannot agree as to any matter vital to the interest of the client, the conflict of opinion should be frankly stated to him for his final determination. His decision should be accepted unless the nature of the difference makes it impracticable for the lawyer whose judgment has been overruled to cooperate effectively. In this event it is his duty to ask the client to relieve him.

Efforts, direct or indirect, in any way to encroach upon the professional employment of another lawyer, are unworthy of those who should be brethren at the Bar; but, nevertheless, it is the right of any lawyer, without fear or favor, to give proper advice to those seeking relief against unfaithful or neglectful counsel, generally after communication with the lawyer of whom the complaint is made.

8. ADVISING UPON THE MERITS OF A CLIENT'S CAUSE

A lawyer should endeavor to obtain full knowledge of his client's cause before advising thereon, and he is bound to give a candid opinion of the merits and probable result of pending or contemplated litigation. The miscarriages to which justice is subject, by reason of surprises and disappointments in evidence and witnesses, and through mistakes of juries and errors of Courts, even though only occasional, admonish lawyers to beware of bold and confident assurances to clients, especially where the employment may depend upon such assurance. Whenever the controversy will admit of fair adjustment, the client should be advised to avoid or to end the litigation.

9. NEGOTIATIONS WITH OPPOSITE PARTY

A lawyer should not in any way communicate upon the subject of controversy with a party represented by counsel; much less should he undertake to negotiate or compromise the matter with him, but should deal only with his counsel. It is incumbent upon the lawyer most particularly to avoid everything that may tend to mislead a party not represented by counsel, and he should not undertake to advise him as to the law.

10. ACQUIRING INTEREST IN LITIGATION

The lawyer should not purchase any interest in the subject-matter of the litigation which he is conducting.

11. DEALING WITH TRUST PROPERTY

The lawyer should refrain from any action whereby for his personal benefit or gain he abuses or takes advantage of the confidence reposed in him by his client.

Money of the client or collected for the client, or other trust property coming into the possession of the lawyer should be reported and accounted for promptly, and should not under any circumstances be commingled with his own or be used by him.

12. Fixing the Amount of the Fee

In fixing fees, lawyers should avoid charges which over-estimate their advice and services, as well as those which undervalue them. A client's ability to pay cannot justify a charge in excess of the value of the service, though his poverty may require a less charge, or even none at all. The reasonable requests of brother lawyers, and of their widows and orphans without ample means, should receive special and kindly consideration.

In determining the amount of the fee, it is proper to consider: (1) the time and labor required, the novelty and difficulty of the questions involved and the skill requisite properly to conduct the cause; (2) whether the acceptance of employment in the particular case will preclude the lawyer's appearance for others in cases likely to arise out of the transaction, and in which there is a reasonable expectation that otherwise he would be employed, or will involve the loss of other employment while employed in the particular case or antagonisms with other clients; (3) the customary charges of the Bar for similar services; (4) the amount involved in the controversy and the benefits resulting to the client from the services; (5) the contingency or the certainty of the compensation; and (6) the character of the employment, whether casual or for an established and constant client. No one of these considerations in itself is controlling. They are mere guides in ascertaining the real value of the service.

In determining the customary charges of the Bar for similar services, it is proper for a lawyer to consider a schedule of minimum fees adopted by a Bar Association, but no lawyer should permit himself to be controlled thereby or follow it as his sole guide in determining the amount of his fee.

In fixing fees it should never be forgotaen that the profession is a branch of the administration of justice and not a mere money-getting trade.

13. Contingent Fees

A contract for a contingent fee, where sanctioned by law,

should be reasonable under all the circumstances of the case, including the risk and uncertainty of the compensation, but should always be subject to the supervision of a Court as to its reasonableness.

14. Suing a Client for a Fee

Controversies with clients concerning compensation are to be avoided by the lawyer so far as shall be compatible with his self-respect and with his right to receive reasonable recompense for his services; and lawsuits with clients should be resorted to only to prevent injustice, imposition or fraud.

15. How far a Lawyer May Go in Supporting a Client's Cause

Nothing operates more certainly to create or to foster popular prejudice against lawyers as a class, and to deprive the profession of that full measure of public esteem and confidence which belongs to the proper discharge of its duties than does the false claim, often set up by the unscrupulous in defense of the questionable transactions, that it is the duty of the lawyer to do whatever may enable him to succeed in winning his client's cause.

It is improper for a lawyer to assert in argument his personal belief in his client's innocence or in the justice of his cause.

The lawyer owes "entire devotion to the interest of the client, warm zeal in the maintenance and defense of his rights and the exertion of his utmost learning and ability," to the end that nothing be taken or be withheld from him, save by the rules of law, legally applied. No fear of judicial disfavor or public unpopularity should restrain him from the full discharge of his duty. In the judicial forum the client is entitled to the benefit of any and every remedy and defense that is authorized by the law of the land, and he may expect his lawyer to assert every such remedy or defense. But it is steadfastly to be borne in mind that the great trust of the lawyer is to be performed within and not without the bounds of the law. The office of attorney does not permit, much less does it demand of him for any client, violation of law or any manner of fraud or chicane. He must obey his own conscience and not that of his client.

16. RESTRAINING CLIENTS FROM IMPROPRIETIES

A lawyer should use his best efforts to restrain and to prevent his clients from doing those things which the lawyer himself ought not to do, particularly with reference to their conduct towards Courts, judicial officers, jurors, witnesses and suitors. If a client persists in such wrongdoing the lawyer should terminate their relation.

17. ILL FEELING AND PERSONALITIES BETWEEN ADVOCATES

Clients, not lawyers, are the litigants. Whatever may be the ill feeling existing between clients, it should not be allowed to influence counsel in their conduct and demeanor toward each other or toward suitors in the case. All personalities between counsel should be scrupulously avoided. In the trial of a cause it is indecent to allude to the personal peculiarities and idiosyncrasies of counsel on the other side. Personal colloquies between counsel which cause delay and promote unseemly wrangling should also be carefully avoided.

18. TREATMENT OF WITNESSES AND LITIGANTS

A lawyer should always treat adverse witnesses and suitors with fairness and due consideration, and he should never minister to the malevolence or prejudices of a client in the trial or conduct of a cause. The client cannot be made the keeper of the lawyer's conscience in professional matters. He has no right to demand that his counsel shall abuse the opposite party or indulge in offensive personalities. Improper speech is not excusable on the ground that it is what the client would say if speaking in his own behalf.

19. APPEARANCE OF LAWYER AS WITNESS FOR HIS CLIENT

When a lawyer is a witness for his client, except as to merely formal matters, such as the attestation or custody of an instrument and the like, he should leave the trial of the case to other counsel. Except when essential to the ends of justice, a lawyer should avoid testifying in court in behalf of his client.

20. Newspaper Discussion of Pending Litigation

Newspaper publications by a lawyer as to pending or anticipated litigation may interfere with a fair trial in the Courts and otherwse prejudice the due administration of justice. Generally they are to be condemned. If the extreme circumstances of a particular case justify a statement to the public, it is unprofessional to make it anonymously. An ex parte reference to the facts should not go beyond quotation from the records and papers on file in the court; but even in extreme cases it is better to avoid any ex parte statement.

21. Punctuality and Expedition

It is the duty of the lawyer not only to his client, but also to the Courts and to the public, to be punctual in attendance, and to be concise and direct in the trial and disposition of couses.

22. Candor and Fairness

The conduct of the lawyer before the Court and with other lawyers should be characterized by candor and fairness.

It is not candid or fair for the lawyer knowingly to misquote the contents of a paper, the testimony of a witness, the language or the argument of opposing counsel, or the language of a decision or a text-book; or with knowledge of its invalidity, to cite as authority a decision that has been overruled, or a statute that has been repealed; or in argument to assert as a fact that which has not been proved, or in those jurisdictions where a side has the opening and closing arguments to mislead his opponent by concealing or withholding positions in his opening argument upon which his side then intends to rely.

It is unprofessional and dishonorable to deal other than candidly with the facts in taking the statements of witnesses, in drawing affidavits and other documents, and in the presentation of causes.

A lawyer should not offer evidence, which he knows the Court should reject, in order to get the same before the jury by argument for its admissibility, nor should he address to the Judge arguments upon any point not properly halling for determination by him. Neither should he introduce into an argument, addressed to the court, remarks or statements intended to influence the jury or bystanders.

These and all kindred practices are unprofessional and unworthy of an officer of the law charged, as is the lawyer, with the duty of aiding in the administration of justice.

23. ATTITUDE TOWARD JURY

All attempts to curry favor with juries by fawning, flattery, or pretended solicitude for their personal comfort are unprofessional. Suggestions of counsel, looking to the comfort or convenience of jurors, and propositions to dispense with argument, should be made to the Court out of the jury's hearing. A lawyer must never converse privately with jurors about the case; and both before and during the trial he should avoid communicating with them, even as to matters foreign to the cause.

24. RIGHT OF LAWYER TO CONTROL THE INCIDENTS OF THE TRIAL

As to incidental matters pending the trial, not affecting the merits of the cause, or working substantial prejudice to the rights of the client, such as forcing the opposite lawyer to trial when he is under affliction or bereavement; forcing the trial on a particular day to the injury of the opposite lawyer when no harm will result from a trial at a different time; agreeing to an extension of time for signing a bill of exceptions, cross-interrogatories and the like, the lawyer must be allowed to judge. In such matters no client has a right to demand that his counsel shall be illiberal, or that he do anything therein repugnant to his own sense of honor and propriety.

25. TAKING TECHNICAL ADVANTAGE OF OPPOSITE COUNSEL —AGREEMENTS WITH HIM

A lawyer should not ignore known customs or practice of the Bar or of a particular Court, even when the law permits, without giving timely notice to the opposing counsel. As far as possible, important agreements, affecting the rights of clients, should be reduced to writing; but it is dishonorable to avoid performance of an agreement fairly made because it is not reduced to writing, as required by rules of Court.

26. PROFESSIONAL ADVOCACY OTHER THAN BEFORE COURTS

A lawyer openly and in his true character may render professional services before legislative or other bodies, regarding proposed legislation and in advocacy of claims, before departments of government, upon the same principles of ethics which justify his appearance before the Courts; but it is unprofessional for a lawyer so engaged to conceal his attorneyship, or to employ secret personal solicitations, or to use means other than those addressed to the reason and understanding to influence action.

27. ADVERTISING, DIRECT OR INDIRECT

It is unprofessional to solicit professional employment by circulars, advertisements, through touters, or by personal communications or interviews not warranted by personal relations. Indirect advertisements for professional employment, such as furnishing or inspiring newspaper comments, or procuring his photograph to be published in connection with causes in which the lawyer has been or is engaged or concerning the manner of their conduct, the magnitude of the interest involved, the importance of the lawyer's position, and all other like self-laudation, offend the traditions and lower the tone of our profession and are reprehensible; but the customary use of simple professional cards is not improper.

Publication in reputable law lists in a manner consistent with the standards of conduct imposed by these canons of brief biographical and informative data is permissible. Such data must not be misleading and may include only a statement of the lawyer's name and the names of his professional associates; addresses, telephone numbers, cable addresses; branches of the profession practiced; date and place of birth and admission to the Bar; schools attended, with dates of graduation, degrees and other educational distinctions; public or quasi-public offices; posts of honor; legal authorships;

legal teaching positions; memberships and offices in bar associations and committees thereof, in legal and scientific societies and legal fraternities; the fact of listings in other reputable law lists; the names and address of references; and, with their written consent, the names of clients regularly represented. A certificate of compliance with the Rules and Standards issued by the Special Committee of Law Lists may be treated as evidence that such list is reputable.

It is not improper for a lawyer who is admitted to practice as a proctor in admiralty to use that designation on his letterhead or shingle or for a lawyer who has complied with the statutory requirements of admission to practice before the patent office to use the designation "patent attorney" or "patent lawyer" or "trade-mark attorney" or "trade-mark lawyer" or any combination of those terms.

28. STIRRING UP LITIGATION, DIRECTLY OR THROUGH AGENTS

It is unprofessional for a lawyer to volunteer advice to bring a lawsuit, except in rare cases where ties of blood, relationship or trust make it his duty to do so. Stirring up strife and litigation is not only unprofessional, but it is indictable at common law. It is disreputable to hunt up defects in titles or other causes of action and inform thereof in order to be employed to bring suit or collect judgment, or to breed litigation by seeking out those with claims for personal injuries or those having any other grounds of action in order to secure them as clients, or to employ agents or runners for like purposes, or to pay or reward, directly or indirectly, those who bring or influence the bringing of such cases to his office, or to remunerate policemen, court or prison officials, physicians, hospital attaches or others who may succeed, under the guise of giving disinterested friendly advice, in influencing the criminal, the sick and the injured, the ignorant or others, to seek his professional services. A duty to the public and to the profession devolves upon every member of the Bar, having knowledge of such practices upon the part of any practitioner, immediately to inform thereof to the end that the offender may be disbarred.

29. Upholding the Honor of the Profession

Lawyers should expose without fear or favor before the proper tribunals corrupt or dishonest conduct in the profession, and should accept without hesitation employment against a member of the Bar who has wronged his client. The counsel upon the trial of a cause in which perjury has been committed owe it to the profession and to the public to bring the matter to the knowledge of the prosecuting authorities. The lawyer should aid in guarding the Bar against the admission to the profession of candidates unfit or unqualified because deficient in either moral character or education. He should strive at all times to uphold the honor and to maintain the dignity of the profession and to improve not only the law but the administration of justice.

30. Justifiable and Unjustifiable Litigations

The lawyer must decline to conduct a civil cause or to make a defense when convinced that it is intended merely to harass or to injure the opposite party or to work oppression or wrong. But otherwise it is his right, and, having accepted retainer, it becomes his duty to insist upon the judgment of the Court as to the legal merts of his client's claim. His appearance in Court should be deemed equivalent to an assertion on his honor that in his opinion his client's case is one proper for judicial determination.

31. Responsibility for Litigation

No lawyer is obliged to act either as adviser or advocate for every person who may wish to become his client. He has the right to decline employment. Every lawyer upon his own responsibility must decide what employment he will accept as counsel, what causes he will bring into Court for plaintiffs, what cases he will contest in Court for defendants. The responsibility for advising questionable transactions, for bringing questionable suits, for urging questionable defenses, is the lawyer's responsibility. He cannot escape it by urging as an excuse that he is only following his client's instructions.

32. The Lawyer's Duty in Its Last Analysis

No client, corporate or individual, however powerful, nor any cause, civil or political, however important, is entitled to receive, nor should any lawyer render, any service or advice involving disloyalty to the law whose ministers we are, or disrespect of the judicial office, which we are bound to uphold, or corruption of any person or persons exercising a public office or private trust, or deception or betrayal of the public. When rendering any such improper service or advice, the lawyer invites and merits stern and just condemnation. Correspondingly, he advances the honor of his profession and the best interests of his client when he renders service or gives advice tending to impress upon the client and his undertaking exact compliance with the strictest principles of moral law. He must also observe and advise his client to observe the statute law, though until a statute shall have been construed and interpreted by competent adjudication, he is free and is entitled to advise as to its validity and as to what he conscientiously believes to be its just meaning and extent. But above all a lawyer will find his highest honor in a deserved reputation for fidelity to private trust and to public duty, as an honest man and as a patriotic and loyal citizen.

33. Partnerships—Names

Partnerships among lawyers for the practice of their profession are very common and are not to be condemned. In the formation of partnerships and the use of partnership names, care should be taken not to violate any law, custom or rule of court locally applicable. Where partnerships are formed between lawyers who are not all admitted to practice in the courts of the state, care should be taken to avoid any misleading name or representation which would create a false impression as to the professional position or privileges of the member not locally admitted. In the formation of partnerships for the practice of law, no person should be admitted or hel dout as a practitioner or member who is not a member of the legal profession, duly authorized to practice, and amenable to professional discipline. In the selection and use of a firm name, no false, misleading, assumed or trade name should be used. The continued use of the name of a deceased or former partner when permissible by local custom, is not unethical, but care should be taken that no imposition or deception is practiced through this use. When a member of the firm, on becoming a judge, is precluded from practicing law, his name should not be continued in the firm name.

Partnerships between lawyers and members of other professions or nonprofessional persons should not be formed or permitted where any part of the partnership's employment consists of the practice of law.

34. DIVISION OF FEES

No division of fees for legal services is proper, except with another lawyer, based upon a division of service or responsibility.

35. INTERMEDIARIES

The professional services of a lawyer should not be controlled or exploited by any lay agency, personal or corporate, which intervenes between client and lawyer. A lawyer's responsibilities and qualifications are individual. He should avoid all relations which direct the performance of his duties by or in the interest of such intermediary. A lawyer's relation to his client should be personal, and the responsibility should be direct to the client. Charitable societies rendering aid to the indigent are not deemed such intermediaries.

A lawyer may accept employment from any organization, such as an association, club or trade organization, to render legal services in any matter in which the organization, as an entity, is interested, but this employment should not include the rendering of legal services to the members of such an organization in respect to their individual affairs.

36. Retirement from Judicial Position or Public Employment

A lawyer should not accept employment as an advocate in any matter upon the merits of which he has previously acted in a judicial capacity.

A lawyer, having once held public office or having been in the public employ, should not after his retirement accept employment in connection with any matter which he has investigated or passed upon while in such office or employ.

37. Confidences of a Client

It is the duty of a lawyer to preserve his client's confidences. This duty outlasts the lawyer's employment, and extends as well to his employees; and neither of them should accept employment which involves or may involve the disclosure or use of these confidences, either for the private advantage of the lawyer or his employees or to the disadvantage of the lawyer or his employees or to the disadvantage of the client, without his knowledge and consent, and even though there are other available sources of such information. A lawyer should not continue employment when he discovers that this obligation prevents the performance of his full duty to his former or to his new client.

If a lawyer is accused by his client, he is not precluded from disclosing the truth in respect to the accusation. The announced intention of a client to commit a crime is not included within the confidences which he is bound to respect. He may properly make such disclosures as may be necessary to prevent the act or protect those against whom it is threatened.

38. Compensation, Commissions and Rebates

A lawyer should accept no compensation, commissions, rebates, or other anvantages fromo thers without the knowlenge and consent of his client after full disclosure.

39. Witnesses

A lawyer may properly interview any witness or prospective witness for the opposing side in any civil or criminal action without the consent of opposing counsel or party.

In doing so, however, he should scrupulously avoid any suggestion calculated to induce the witness to suppress or deviate from the truth, or in any degree to affect his free and untrammeled conduct when appearing at the trial or on the witness stand.

40. NEWSPAPERS
A lawyer may with propriety write articles for publications in which he gives information upon the law; but he should not accept employment from such publications to advise inquirers in respect to their individual rights.

41. DISCOVERY OF IMPOSITION AND DECEPTION
When a lawyer discovers that some fraud or deception has been practiced, which has unjustly imposed upon the Court or a party, he should endeavor to rectify it; at first by advising his client, and if his client refuses to forego the advantage thus unjustly gained, he should promptly inform the injured person or his counsel, so that they may take appropriate steps.

42. EXPENSES
A lawyer may not properly agree with a client that the lawyer shall pay or bear the expenses of litigation; he may in good faith advance expenses as matter of convenience, but subject to reimbursement.

43. APPROVED LAW LISTS
It is improper for a lawyer to permit his name to be published in a law list the conduct, management or contents of which are calculated or likely to deceive or injure the public or the profession, or to lower the dignity or standing of the profession.

44. WITHDRAWAL FROM EMPLOYMENT AS ATTORNEY OR COUNSEL
The right of an attorney or counsel to withdraw from employment, once assumed, arises only from good cause. Even the desire or consent of the client is not always sufficient. The lawyer should not throw up the unfinished task to the detriment of his client, except for reasons of honor or self-

respect. If the client insists upon an unjust or immoral course in the conduct of his case, or if he persists over the attorney's remonstrance in presenting frivolous defenses, or if he deliberately disregards an agreement or obligation as to fees or expenses, the lawyer may be warranted in withdrawing on due notice to the client, allowing him time to employ another lawyer. So also when a lawyer discovers that his client has no case and the client is determined to continue it; or even if the lawyer finds himself incapable of conducting the case effectively. Sundry other instances may arise in which withdrawal is to be justified. Upon withdrawing from a case after a retainer has been paid, the attorney should refund such part of the retainer as has not been clearly earned.

45. SPECIALISTS

The canons of the American Bar Association apply to all branches of the legal profession; specialists in particular branches are not to be considered as exempt from the application of these principles.

46. NOTICE OF SPECIALIZED LEGAL SERVICE

Where a lawyer is engaged in rendering a specialized legal service directly and only to other lawyers, a brief, dignified notice of that fact, couched in language indicating that it is addressed to lawyers, inserted in legal periodicals and like publications, when it will afford convenient and beneficial information to lawyers desiring to obtain such service, is not improper.

47. AIDING THE UNAUTHORIZED PRACTICE OF LAW

No lawyer shall permit his professional services, or his name, to be used in aid of, or to make possible, the unauthorized practice of law by any lay agency, personal or corporate.

OATH OF ADMISSION

The general principles which should ever control the lawyer in the practice of his profession are clearly set forth in the following Oath of Admission to the Bar, formulated upon that in use in the State of Washington, and which conforms in its main outlines to the "duities" of lawyers as defined by statutory enactments in that and many other States of the Union—duties which they are sworn on admission to obey and for the wilful violation of which disbarment is provided.

I DO SOLEMNLY SWEAR:

I will support the Constitution of the United States and the Constitution of the State of ....;

I will maintain the respect due to Courts of Justice and judicial officers;

I will not counsel or maintain any suit or proceeding which shall appear to me to be unjust, nor any defense except such as I believe to be honestly debatable under the law of the land;

I will employ for the purpose of maintaining the causes confided to me such means only as are consistent with truth and honor, and will never seek to mislead the Judge or jury by any artifice or false statement of fact or law;

I will maintain the confidence and preserve inviolate the secrets of my client, and will accept no compensation in connection with his business except from him or with his knowledge and approval;

I will abstain from all offensive personality, and advance no fact prejudicial to the honor or reputation of a party or witness, unless required by the justice of the cause with which I am charged.

I will never reject, from any consideration personal to myself, the cause of the defenseless or oppressed, or delay any man's cause for lucre or malice. SO HELP ME GOD.

We commend this form of oath for adoption by the proper authorities in all the States and Territories.

BIBLIOGRAPHY

Abbott, Austin. Abbott's criminal trial practice. Rochester, N. Y., Lawyers co-operative, 1939

Abbott, Austin. A brief for the trial of civil issues before a jury. Rochester, N. Y., Lawyers co-operative, 1935.

Abbott, Austin. Trial evidence. New York, Baker, Voorhis, 1931.

Alfange, Dean. The Supreme Court and the national will. Garden City, N. Y., Doubleday, Doran, 1937.

Allen, Frederick James. The law as a vocation. Cambridge, Mass., Harvard university press, 1919.

American Academy of Political and Social Science, Philadelphia. Civil rights in America, edited by Robert K. Carr. Philadelphia, 1951.

American Academy of Political and Social Science. Philadelphia. Internal security and civil rights, edited by Thorsten Sellin. Philadelphia, 1955.

American Academy of Political and Social Science. Philadelphia. Judicial administration and the common man, edited by Benjamin Kaplan and Livingston Hall. Philadelphia, 1953.

American Bar Association. Standards of the American bar association for legal education. Chicago, 1943.

American Bar Association. Section of Judicial Administration. The improvement of the administration of justice. Washington, 1952.

American Law Institute. Model code of evidence as adopted and promulgated by the American Law Institute at Philadelphia, Pa. May 1942.

Andrews, Charles McLean. The colonial period of American history. New Haven, Yale university press, 1934. 4v.

Andrews, James DeWitt. American law: a commentary on the jurisprudence, Constitution and laws of the United States. Chicago, Callaghan, 1908.

Association of the Bar of the City of New York. Bad housekeeping; the administration of the New York Courts. New York, 1955.

Aumann, Francis Robert. The changing American legal system. Columbus, Ohio State university press, 1940.

Aumann, Francis Robert. The instrumentalities of justice: their forms, functions, and limitations. Columbus, Ohio State university press, 1956.

Aycock, William B. Military law under the Uniform code of military justice. Chapel Hill, University of North Carolina press, 1955.

Bacon, Charles William. The American plan of government; the Constitution of the United States as interpreted by accepted authorities. New York, Putnam, 1921.

Bacon, Charles William. The reasonableness of the law; the adaptability of legal sanctions to the needs of society. New York, Putnam, 1924.

Barrows, Chester Leonard. William M. Evarts, lawyer, diplomat, statesman. Chapel Hill, University of North Carolina press, 1941.

Bates, Ernest Sutherland. The story of the Supreme Court. Indianapolis, Bobbs-Merrill, 1936.

Beaney, William Merritt. The right to counsel in American courts. Ann Arbor, University of Michigan press, 1955.

Beard, Charles Austin. An economic interpretation of the Constitution. New York, Macmillan, 1923.

Berger, Morroe. Equality by statute; legal controls over group discrimination. New York, Columbia university press, 1952.

Beveridge, Albert Jeremiah. The life of John Marshall. Boston, Houghton Mifflin, 1916-19.

Bliss, Edward N. Defense investigation. Springfield, Ill., Thomas, 1956.
Blume, William Wirt. American civil procedure. Englewood Cliffs, N. J., Prentice-Hall, 1955.
Botein, Bernard. Trial judge; the candid, behind-the-bench story of Justice Bernard Botein. New York, Simon and Schuster, 1952.
Bowen, Catherine (Drinker). Yankee from Olympus; Justice Holmes and his family. Boston, Little, Brown, 1944.
Bowie, Robert Richardson. Studies in federalism. Boston, Little, Brown, 1954.
Bradway, John Saeger. Legal aid clinic instruction at Duke university. Durham, N. C., Duke university press, 1944.
Bradway, John Saeger. Legal aid bureaus, their organization and administration. Chicago, Public administration service, 1937.
Brand, George Edward. Bar associations, attorneys and judges: organization, ethics and discipline. Chicago, American judicature society, 1956.
Brant, Irving. James Madison. Indianapolis, Bobbs-Merrill, 1941.
Brigance, William Norwood. Jeremiah Sullivan Black, a defender of the Constitution and the Ten commandments. Philadelphia, University of Pennsylvania press, 1934.
Brown, Esther Lucile. Lawyers and the promotion of justice. New York, Russell Sage Foundation, 1938.
Brown, Esther Lucile. Lawyers, law schools and the public service. New York, Russell Sage Foundation, 1948.
Brown, Robert Eldon. Charles Beard and the Constitution, a critical analysis of "An economic interpretation of the Constitution." Princeton, Princeton university press, 1956.
Brownell, Emery A. Legal aid in the United States. Rochester, N. Y., Lawyers co-operative, 1951.
Bunn, Charles Wilson. A brief survey of the jurisdiction and practice of the courts of the United States. St. Paul, West, 1949.
Cahill, Fred V. Judicial legislation. New York, Ronald, 1952.
Callender, Clarence N. American courts; their organization and procedure. New York, McGraw-Hill, 1927.
Carpenter, William Seal. Judicial tenure in the United States. New Haven, Yale university press, 1918.
Carr, Robert Kenneth. Federal protection of civil rights. Ithaca, Cornell university press, 1947.
Chafee, Zechariah. The blessings of liberty. Philadelphia, Lippincott, 1956.
Chafee, Zechariah. How human rights got into the Constitution. Boston, Boston university press, 1952.
Chestnut, W. Calvin. A federal judge sums up. Baltimore, Daily record, 1947.
Conrad, Earl. Mr. Seward for the defense. New York, Rinehart, 1956.
Corwin, Edward Samuel. The Constitution and what it means today. Princeton, Princeton university press, 1946.
Corwin, Edward Samuel. Court ofev Constitution; a study of judicial review as an instrument of popular government. New York, Smith, 1950.
Corwin, Edward Samuel. The twilight of the Supreme court; a history of our constitutional theory. New Haven, Yale university press, 1934.
Crosskey, William Winslow. Politics and the Constitution in the history of the United States. Chicago, University of Chicago press, 1953.
Curtis, Charles Pelham. It's your law. Cambridge, Mass., Harvard university press, 1954.
Cushman, Robert Eugene. Civil liberties in the United States. Ithaca, Cornell university press, 1956.
Daniel, Hawthorne. Judge Medina, a biography. New York, Funk, 1952.
Depew, Chauncey Mitchell. My memories of eighty years. New York, Scribner, 1922.

Douglass, Paul Franklin. The justice of the peace courts of Hamilton County, Ohio. Baltimore. Johns Hopkins press, 1932.

Douglass, Paul Franklin. The mayor's courts of Hamilton County, Ohio. Baltimore. Johns Hopkins press, 1933.

Drinker, Henry Sandwith. Legal ethics. New York, Columbia university press, 1953.

Duke University. School of Law. Committee on pre-legal education of the law faculty. Undergraduate preparation for the study of law. Durham, 1950.

Dumbauld, Edward. The Bill of Rights and what it means today. Norman, University of Oklahoma press, 1957.

Dunham, Allison. Mr. Justice, edited by Allison Dunham and Philip B. Kurland. Chicago, University of Chicago press, 1956.

Edwards, Newton. The courts and the public schools. Chicago, University of Chicago press, 1955.

Fairman, Charles. Mr. Justice Miller and the Supreme court, 1862-1890. Cambridge, Mass., Harvard university press, 1939.

Farmer, Frances, ed. The Wilson reader. New York, Oceana, 1956.

The Federalist. The Federalist; a commentary on the Constitution of the United States, being a collection of essays written by Alexander Hamilton, James Madison and John Jay in support of the Constitution agreed upon September 17, 1787, by the Federal convention. New York, Dunne, 1901.

Field, Henry Martyn. The life of David Dudley Field. New York, Scribner, 1898.

Fraenkel, Osmond Kessler. Our civil liberties. New York, Viking, 1944.

Frank, Jerome. Courts on trial; myth and reality in American justice. Princeton, Princeton university press, 1949.

Frank, John Paul. Mr. Justice Black, the man and his opinions. Introduction by Charles A. Beard. New York, Knopf, 1949.

Frankfurter, Felix. The business of the Supreme Court. New York, Macmillan, 1927.

Frankfurter, Felix. Mr. Justice Holmes and the Supreme court. Cambridge, Mass., Harvard university press, 1938.

Fuess, Claude Moore. Rufus Choate, the wizard of the law. New York, Minton, Balch, 1928.

Gardner, Erle Stanley. The court of last resort. New York, Sloane Associates, 1952.

Gavit, Bernard Campbell. Introduction to the study of law. Brooklyn, Foundation press, 1951.

Glueck, Sheldon. Crime and justice. Boston, Little, Brown, 1936.

Goldman, Mayer C. The public defender: a necessary factor in the administration of justice. New York, Putnam, 1919.

Griswold, Erwin N. The 5th amendment today. Cambridge, Harvard university press, 1955.

Haines, Charles Grove. The American doctrine of judicial supremacy. Berkeley, Calif., University of California press, 1932.

Hamlin, Paul Mahlon. Legal education in colonial New York. New York, New York university press, 1939.

Hammonds, Oliver Wendell. The attorney general in the American colonies. New York, New York University School of Law, 1939.

Harno, Albert James. Legal education in the United States; a report prepared for the Survey of the Legal Profession. San Francisco, Bancroft-Whitney, 1953.

Haynes, Evan. The selection and tenure of judges. Newark, N. J., The national conference of judicial councils, 1944.

Hays, Arthur Garfield. City lawyer; the autobiography of a law practice. New York, Simon and Schuster, 1942.

Heller, Francis Howard. The Sixth amendment to the Constitution of the
    United States; a study in constitutional development. Lawrence, University of Kansas press, 1951.
Hendel, Samuel. Charles Evans Hughes and the Supreme Court. New
    York, King's Crown press, 1951.
Hendrick, Burton Jesse. Bulwark of the republic: a biography of the Constitution. Boston, Little, Brown, 1937.
Hook, Sidney. Common sense and the fifth amendment. New York, Criterion books, 1957.
Housel, Theodore Wardle and Walser, Guy O. Defending and prosecuting
    federal criminal cases. Buffalo, Dennis, 1946.
Howe, Mark De Wolfe. Justice Oliver Wendell Holmes. Cambridge,
    Belknap press of Harvard university press, 1957-
Howe, Mark De Wolfe. Readings in American legal history. Cambrirdge,
    Mass., Harvard university press, 1949.
Hurst, James Willard. Law and the conditions of freedom in the nineteenth century United States. Madison, Wisconsin, University of
    Wisconsin press, 1956.
Inbau, Fred Edward. Self-incrimination: what can an accused person be
    compelled to do? Springfield, Ill., Thomas, 1950.
Jackson, Robert Houghwout. The struggle for judicial supremacy; a study
    of a crisis in American power politics. New York, Knopf, 1941.
Jones, William Melville. Chief Justice John Marshall; a reappraisal.
    Ithaca, N. Y., Published for College of William and Mary by Cornell
    university press, 1956.
Keeney, Barnaby Conrad. Judgment by peers. Cambridge, Harvard university press, 1949.
King, Willard Leroy. Melville Weston Fuller, Chief Justice of the United
    States, 1888-1910. New York, Macmillan, 1950.
Kinnane, Charles Herman. A first book on Anglo-American law. Indianapolis, Bobbs-Merrill, 1952.
Knox, John Clark. A judge comes of age. New York, Scribner, 1940.
Konefsky, Samuel Joseph. Chief Justice Stone and the Supreme Court.
    New York, Macmillan, 1945.
Konvitz, Milton Ridvas. Bill of rights reader: leading constitutional cases.
    Ithaca, Cornell university press, 1954.
Konvitz, Milton Ridvas. The Constitution and civil rights. New York,
    Columbia university press, 1947.
Lasson, Nelson Bernard. The history and development of the fourth
    amendment to the United States Constitution. Baltimore, John Hopkins press, 1937.
Lasswell, Harold Dwight. National security and individual freedom. New
    York, McGraw-Hill, 1950.
Legal Aid Society, New York. Annual reports. New York, 1877-
Lehman, Irving. The influence of Judge Cardozo on the common law.
    Garden City, N. Y., Doubleday, Doran, 1942.
Leopold, Richard William. Elihu Root and the conservative tradition.
    Boston, Little, Brown, 1954.
Lepawsky, Albert. The judicial system of metropolitan Chicago. Chicago,
    University of Chicago press, 1932.
Levy, Leonard Williams. The law of the Commonwealth and Chief Justice Shaw. Cambridge, Harvard university press, 1957.
Lewis, Edmund H. The contribution of Judge Irving Lehman to the development of the law. New York, Association of the Bar of the City
    of New York, 1951.
Lewis, William Draper. Interpreting the Constitution. Charlottesville, Virginia, Michie, 1937.

Lief, Alfred. Brandeis; the personal history of an American ideal. New York, Stackpole, 1936.

Loth, David Goldsmith. Chief Justice; John Marshall and the growth of the republic. New York, Norton, 1949.

McCart, Samuel W. What every person should know about jury trials. New York, Vantage press, 1953.

McGehee, Lucius Polk. Due process of the law under the federal Constitution. Northport, Long Island, N. Y., Edward Thompson, 1906.

Machen, Ernest William. The law of search and seizure. Chapel Hill, Institute of government, University of North Carolina, 1950.

Maguire, John MacArthur. Evidence; common sense and common law. Chicago, Foundation press, 1947.

Marke, Julius J., ed. The Holmes reader; the life, writings, speeches, constitutional decisions, etc., of the late Oliver Wendel Homles . . . as well as an evaluation of his work and achievements by eminent authorities. New York, Oceana, 1955.

Mason, Alpheus Thomas. Harlan Fiske Stone: pillar of the law. New York, Viking press, 1956.

Mayers, Lewis. The American legal system. New York, Harper, 1955.

Michael, Jerome and Adler, Mortimer. The nature of judicial proof; an inquiry into the logical, legal and empirical aspects of the law of evidence. New York, The Ad press, 1931.

Millar, Robert Wyness. Civil procedure of the trial court in historical perspective. New York, Law Center of New York University for the National Conference of Judicial Councils, 1952.

Miller, Helen Day (Hill). George Mason, constitutionalist. Cambridge, Mass., Harvard university press, 1938.

Mr. Justice Brandeis; essays by Charles E. Hughes, Max Lerner, Felix Frankfurter . . . [and others] edited by Felix Frankfurter, with an introduction by Oliver Wendell Holmes. New Haven, Yale university press, 1932.

Moley, Raymond. Our criminal courts. New York, Minton, Balch, 1930.

Moley, Raymond. Politics and criminal prosecution. New York, Minton, Balch, 1929.

Moore, James William. Federal practice. Albany, Bender, 1932.

Newman, Edwin S., ed. The freedom reader. New York, Oceana, 1955.

Newman, Edwin S. The law of civil rights and civil liberties. New York, Oceana, 1949.

Norton, Thomas James. The Constitution of the United States, its sources and its application. Cleveland, World Publishing, 1940.

Ohlinger, Gustavus. Jurisdiction and procedure of the courts of the United States. Cincinnati, Anderson, 1948-56.

O'Neill, James Milton. Religion and education under the Constitution. New York, Harper, 1949.

Orfield, Lester Bernhardt. Criminal procedure from arrest to appeal. New York, New York university press, 1947.

Osgood, Herbert Levi. The American colonies in the seventeenth century. New York, Macmillan, 1904.

Osgood, Herbert Levi. The American colonies in the eighteenth century. New York, Columbia university press, 1924.

Palmer, Benjamin Whipple. Marshall and Taney; statesmen of the law. Minneapolis, University of Minnesota press, 1939.

Partridge, Bellamy. Country lawyer. New York, Mc-Graw-Hill, 1939.

Paschal, Joel Francis. Mr. Justice Sutherland, a man against the State. Princeton, Princeton university press, 1951.

Patterson, Caleb Perry. The constitutional principles of Thomas Jefferson. Austin, University of Texas press, 1953.

Phillips, Orie L. Conduct of judges and lawyers; a study of the professional ethics, discipline and disbarment. Los Angeles, Published for the Survey of the legal profession by Parker, 1952.

Philos, Conrad D. Handbook of court martial law. Chicago, Callaghan, 1951.

Pollack, Ervin Harold, ed. The Brandeis reader; the life and contributions of Mr. Justice Louis D. Brandeis, edited with commentary. New York, Oceana, 1956.

Pollard, Joseph Percival. Mr. Justice Cardozo; a liberal mind in action. New York, Yorktown press, 1935.

Porter, Charles Orlando. Lawyer reference plans. Boston, Survey of the legal profession, 1949.

Pound, Roscoe. Appellate procedure in civil cases. Boston, Little, Brown, 1941.

Pound, Roscoe. Criminal justice in America. New York, Holt, 1930.

Pound, Roscoe. The lawyer from antiquity to modern times, with particular reference to the development of bar associations in the United States. St. Paul, West, 1953.

Pound, Roscoe. Organization of courts. Boston, Little, Brown, 1940.

Pringle, Henry Fowles. The life and times of William Howard Taft. New York, Farrar & Rinehart, 1939.

Pusey, Merlo John. Charles Evans Hughes. New York, Macmillan, 1951.

Puttkammer, Ernst Wilfred. Administration of criminal law. Chicago, University of Chicago press, 1953.

Radin, Max. Handbook of Anglo-American legal history. St. Paul, West, 1936.

Read, Conyers, ed. The constitution reconsidered. New York, Columbia university press, 1938.

Redden, Kenneth Robert. An introductory survey of the place of law in our civilization. Charlottesville, Va., Michie, 1946.

Reed, Alfred Zantzinger. Present day law schools in the United States. New York, The Carnegie foundation for the advancement of teaching, 1928.

Reed, Alfred Zantzinger. Training for the public profession of the law. New York, Scribner, 1921.

Reppy, Alison. Civil rights in the United States. New York, Central Book, 1951.

Reynolds, Quentin James. Courtroom, the story of Samuel S. Leibowitz. New York, Farrar, Straus, 1950.

Roberts, Owen Josephus. The Court and the Constitution. Cambridge, Harvard university press, 1951.

Robertson, Reynolds and Kirkman, Francis R. Jurisdiction of the Supreme Court of the United States. Albany, Bender, 1951.

Rothe, Bertha M., ed. Daniel Webster reader. New York, Oceana publications, 1956.

Rutland, Robert Allen. The birth of the Bill of Rights, 1776-1791. Chapel Hill, University of North Carolina press, 1955.

Schwartzman, Ruth. Law of personal liberties. New York, Oceana publications, 1955.

Scott, James Brown. Judicial settlement of controversies between states of the American union. Oxford, Clarendon press, 1919.

Shartel, Burke. Our legal system and how it operates. Ann Arbor, University of Michigan press, 1951.

Shientag, Bernard Lloyd. The personality of the judge. New York, Association of the Bar of the city of New York, the committee on post admission legal education, 1944.

Smith, Charles Page. James Wilson, founding father, 1742-1798. Chapel Hill, University of North Carolina press for the Institute of Early American History and Culture, 1956.

Smith, Reginald Heber. Justice and the poor . . . with particular reference to legal aid work in the United States. New York, The Carnegie foundation for the advancement of teaching, 1919.

Smith, Reginald Heber. Legal service offices for persons of moderate means. Boston, Survey of the Legal Profession, 1950.

Snedeker, James. Military justice under the Uniform code. Boston, Little, Brown, 1953.

Surrency, Erwin C., ed. The Marshall reader; the life and contributions of Chief Justice John Marshall. New York, Oceana, 1955.

Swisher, Carl Brent. Roger B. Taney. New York, Macmillan, 1935.

Swisher, Carl Brent. Stephen J. Field, craftsman of the law. Washington, Brookings institution, 1930.

Ten Broek, Jacobus. The anti-slavery origins of the Fourteenth amendment. Berkeley, University of California press, 1951.

Thorpe, Frances Newton. The Federal and State constitutions, colonial charters, and other organic laws of the states, territories and colonies. Washington, Gov't. print. off., 1909. 7 v.

Tweed, Harrison. The Legal Aid Society, New York City, 1876-1951. New York, Legal aid society, 1954.

Umbreit, Kenneth Bernard. Our eleven chief justices; a history of the Supreme court in terms of their personalities. New York, Harper, 1938.

UNESCO. University teaching in the social sciences: Law. New York, Columbia university press, 1954.

United States. Constitution. The Constitution of the United States. Analysis and interpretation: annotaions of cases decided by he Supreme Court of the United States to June 30, 1952. Washington, Gov't. print. off., 1953.

Vanderbilt, Arthur T. The challenge of law reform. Princeton, Princeton university press, 1955.

Vanderbilt, Arthur T. Judges and juries: their functions, qualifications and selection. Boston, Boston university press, 1956.

Vanderbilt, Arthur T. Minimum standards of judicial administration. New York, Law center of New York university, 1949.

Von Moschzisker, Robert. Trial by jury: a brief review of its origin, development and merits, and discussion of actual conduct of jury trials. Philadelphia, Bisel, 1930.

Warren, Charles. A history of the American bar. Boston, Little, Brown, 1911.

Warren, Charles. The making of the Constitution. Boston, Little, Brown, 1928.

Warren, Charles. The Supreme Court in United States history. Boston, Little, Brown, 1922. 3v.

Wendell, Mitchell. Relations between the Federal and State courts. New York, Columbia university press, 1949.

Wigmore, John Henry. A students' textbook of the law of evidence. Chicago, Foundation press, 1935.

Wood, Virginia L. Due process of law, 1932-1949. Baton Rouge, Louisiana State university press, 1951.

Wyzanski, Charles Edward. A trial judge's freedom and responsibility. New York, Association of the Bar of the City of New York, 1952.

INDEX